Public & Banking
Debt
is just an
Illusion

Debt is just an Illusion

Debt is just an Illusion

Copyright © 2021 Randall Earl Kaiser

All rights reserved. No reproduction, copy or transmission of this publication may be made without written permission. Copyright theft is stealing. No paragraph of this publication may be reproduced, copied or transmitted save with written permission from the author or in accordance with the provision of the Copyright. Design and Patents Act 1988, or under the terms of any license permitting limited copying issued by the Copyright Licensing Agency.

Any person who does any unauthorized act in relation to this publication may be liable to criminal prosecution and civil claims for damages. The author has asserted his fight to be identified as the author of this work in accordance with the Copyright, Design and Patents Act 1988.

First published June 2021.

Front Cover: Photograph by Randall Kaiser

Publisher: William Ladic

ISBN -97984-7-6460107

Debt is just an Illusion

Randall Earl Kaiser

Debt is just an Illusion

A gift to you both

Earl Fredrick Kaiser

Pearl Margret Kaiser nee *Hogg*

Contents

Foreword .... *i*
Introduction .... *iii*

1. The Heart of Calgary 1
2. Mayor Randall Earl Kaiser 13
3. Communication is Key! 23
4. Victory Notes 51
5. Filipina 'Gold'en Girls 61
6. Jakarta Gems 75
7. Sulu Sea Collection 93
8. The 'Elite' Bloodline 105
9. Ownership of the People 117
10. Lost Property 139
11. Chinese Whispers 147
12. The Pyramid of Exploitation 165
13. The Retail Value Chain 177
14. Bulldog Rancher 189
15. City Council 209
16. Closer to God 223
17. Splitting Adams 245

A Primise *257*
Afterword *259*
Aramaic Prayer *261*
Acknowledgements *265*

Debt is just an Illusion

Debt is just an Illusion

Debt is just an Illusion

Foreword

Greetings!

My relationship with Randall Earl Kaiser is in friendship but also as the author of this book. Apparently, I would be called a 'ghost writer' but I am no ghost, not invisible or behind the scenes, as you now know who I am!

I have been privileged to co-create this book with Randall. I only accepted the proposal because of the truth, which I believe ALL humans need to know about.

Randall and I worked well together as a team, as he narrated his experiences and I was able to transcribe the words to paper, embracing his personality and soul essence. I have added numerous additions to enhance Randall's experiences and made extensions of my own which I have acquired through my own personal background and involvement on these subjects, exposed throughout the book.

I am so glad that you are here to figure out, interpret, perceive, identify and become more conscious of a bigger truth.

This book is filled with a plethora of data, people and situations, for you to distinguish the difference between one's reality and non-reality.

The truth can be challenging to make sense of, especially when you have done a particular thing or action for a number of decades. Then a

Debt is just an Illusion

modern day detective arrives in your life, who unearths these great mysteries and can explain them in full. But funnily enough, for many people, these 'great mysteries' seem not to be a problem to live with every day or to question why they even exist.

Money is just money.

Or is it?

Everyone has debt.

Everyone has credit.

This sounds basic but it's also untrue.

Our debt becomes our responsibility. It becomes a focus in life, which can weigh down the human soul. This illusion of debt is unwanted, unrequested and undesirable.

No, it's not a puzzle.

This book will have ALL of the information you need about money and much more. It may even be a starting point for you to do some detective work of your own. There are many ways to access the data recorded in this book.

I do advise you to take the book step by step because of its impact of truth and details. You may even have to re-read the book again, to look at things from a different angle.

Enjoy the book!

Danushia Kaczmarek

Debt is just an Illusion

Introduction

Walk with me……as I tell you my story which I began to narrate, on 15th April 2021.

From Rancher to Banker.

I have had the pleasure of conversing with Royalty, Presidents, Mayors and Military Generals. Dined and discussing Politics, Banking and the hidden treasures underground. From Millionaires and Billionaires owning corporations and organisations, to meeting the innocence of young children, begging for money in the streets.

I was a wealthy ranch owner and I too have been a wanderer of the land, without ownership of a home or vehicle, as I move from one destination to another. But I call it LIFE in the fast lane! With endless and unlimited resources, combined with an air of trust in the Divine!

Starting from the present day, we weave back in time to my ancestry.

Debt is just an Illusion

1

The Heart of Calgary

"The speculative episode always ends not with a whimper but with a bang."
~ John Kenneth Galbraith - A Short History of Financial Euphoria ~

My name is Randall Earl Kaiser.

I am currently 60 years of age and I have the privilege of living in a stunning city called Calgary, which is situated in Alberta, Canada. You may see me walking through the city, meditating in the parks and striding through the malls. You may even spot me lounging in the Municipal building or enjoying some food in one of our great eateries! I'm the 6' tall guy with a big smile and I usually adorn myself with my 'White Cowboy' hat, which I wear in all seasons. I have worn many cowboy hats over the decades being a rancher an' all! And in various colours but I am liking the colour white at the moment, as I have never seen a Gold Hat yet, that would suit me!

Even when it's icy cold and the temperature plummets to an almighty -35°C, you probably will catch me with my 'ear muffs' under my Stetson! I'm healthy, enjoy laughter, adventure and I can be very spontaneous by nature. Being healthy is very important to me, as this enables me to enjoy my life moving my body freely, without disease and having the ability to feel able to conquer any challenge that stands in my way, of living the best life that I can, whilst I'm here anyways.

Ten years ago, I recovered from liver cancer and I have never felt as alive as I do right now! I'll dive into that story a little later on but laughter was a big part of that recovery. Finding the joy in life heals a multitude of health imbalances and being adventurous and playful too, as we all possess this quality. If you can't remember this side of yourself, it's always there ready and waiting, for you to explore and play!

I love being outdoors as it gives me a sense of freedom and aliveness. I have an extremely curious mind, which is analytical and absorbent. I have a fondness for observing life around me and having all manner of appreciation of conversations with other people, which adds so much value to my life. Even though I can have my masculine suit on, the soft part of me also exists where I can dive into my reflective side, which enjoys the peaceful times in nature and finding reverence in my solitude, to reflect and recalibrate myself.

Now you know a little more about me before the real stories begin, where I leave no stone unturned for you, throughout the rest of my memoir and journal...But first, I just wish to share with you, the place that I call home.

Where is home for you?

Not everyone feels a sense of belonging somewhere.

Not everyone feels that they can call a place, home.

A home could be a dwelling or residence.

A home could be a family or community.

A home could be living from the heart and not attached to a place or people.

I feel at home in Calgary, my ancestry brought my bloodline here a long time ago. I feel so strongly connected to my roots that I have decided to join the list of candidates to become the next Mayor of Calgary!

I have not yet had the experience of seeing all of the major cities in the world but during my travels over the past few years, I have had some eye-opening and astonishing experiences in Hong Kong, Shanghai, New York, London, Manila and Jakarta. But not one of these cities that are celebrated and renowned for their magnificence, architecture or attractions has come close to the uniqueness that I've found in Calgary, my home. This incredible place is situated in the foothills of the Canadian Rockies and the only way that I can describe it, is that I see it being "so well put together".

What do I mean by this?

Well, you have everything inside and everything outside, from the core inner city to the outermost lands.

If you can imagine standing in a central place, at a single point and you get to view a 360° panoramic scene and everywhere you look, the whole of Calgary unfolds in front of you. How magical is that!

Maybe, when you come to visit in the future, or even if you live here already, I recommend that you get your shoes on and explore the wonders of this beautiful land and grab the opportunity to go and stand at the top of Nose Hill Park. This is one of my regular places that I go to and this range overlooks about 70% of Calgary. It's the fourth largest urban park in Canada and it's claimed to be one of the largest public parks in North America. Truly a place for all and everyone to enjoy! Spread the word about this beautiful and sacred land.

Why do I say it's 'sacred land'?

Because anywhere that is a place on Mother Earth, is sacred.

It has such a tremendous history, this plane-t.

The Earth is our ancestral heritage, which is available to us all to plug ourselves into and it will always be available to celebrate now and for our future generations. Ancestral is not limited to culture, tribe, civilisation, class or lineage. It is all of everything.

You may even ask "What's this got to do with Money, Corporations, Political & Banking 'systems', Debt and Credit, Randall?"

Step by step, my dear. All will be revealed!

Are you ready to go to Nose Hill Park with me?

To see the horizon and beyond?

I do hope so because this is where I got the idea for my book too.

You can tell me what you can see on the horizon and I will point out what you cannot see.

Stand next to me, so that I can show you the wonders in all general directions - north, south, east and west, a 360° bird's eye view!

Imagine that you and I are standing on the peak of Nose Hill Park, at this exact moment. Take a deep breath and feel the freshness of the air. This is what you can see;

- To the North – Parkland, Lakes, Swamps and Trees
- To the South – Foothills and Plaines.
- To the East – Prairie Provinces and native flat country, grasslands and lowlands.
- To the West – The Great Rocky Mountains

I have been told that this park and piece of land, sits upon magnetic and energetic lines which we are unable to see with the naked eye. The lines cross through, under and over the Earth.

You may even come across a well-known landmark which honours the Indigenous people. It is built with stones and is in a geometric formation. It represents a cultural medicine wheel. The people who believe in connecting to the purity and the spirits of our lands, give their offerings and prayers to this wheel of life.

If you were in your car, you could drive around the whole of Calgary and you'd see these four very distinctive environments within sixty minutes!

There are two well-known rivers that run through the city itself, the Bow River and the Elbow River. The Bow River has worldwide fame for Rainbow and Brown trout fly-fishing.

Randall where the Elbow & Bow Rivers Meet

Our wildlife is abundant with rabbits, squirrels, birds, deer, coyote, moose, bats, mink, weasel, black bear, raccoon, skunk, and cougar.

The trees are deciduous and coniferous and have a beautiful magnificence in their size and colour. The flowers, blossoms and fruits are eye-catching wonders of this stunning land. Sometimes the energy and sheer vastness of it all can be so breathtakingly beautiful.

Now, the flatter areas along the river banks are where most of our population lives and further along, we arrive at downtown Calgary. This is designed for the businesses, economy, oil industries, banks, government, council, media communication, the travel industry, infrastructure and educational resources combined with a richness of leisure, multi-cultural and entertainment activities, including the most extensive pathway and bikeway system in the whole of North America. Every year it hosts a multitude of festivals that attract millions of people. It is also claimed to be one of the cleanest, safest and healthiest cities in the world and a leader in the overall quality of life. It is also the administrative and financial headquarters of Canada's petroleum industry.

Back outside the city, we arrive at farm land. Our main industry is with our cattle and agriculture. In 1881, the federal government began to offer leases for cattle-ranching in Alberta and now Calgary celebrates its history as a cattle-ranching capital.

It is a sensational city, during all seasons. It's such a delight to see people enjoying the toboggan and cross-country ski trails with the sound of children's laughter resounding in the air, sensing the families uniting and having fun.

If it's too much of a trek for you to venture out to Nose Hill Park after enjoying the delights of the city, there is always the Prince's Island Park where you can rejuvenate oneself and explore the splendours in the valley.

During the coronavirus lockdown from 2020 until the present day of writing this book, I have noticed more and more beauty and charm arriving in people's gardens, with the owners planting trees, raising their garden beds and enlivening their space, lawns and yards.

Have you noticed what's been going on in your neighbourhood?

Is it your garden that I looked in?

Are you *still* wondering where I am going with all of this?

Well, I have told you of the wonder, beauty and positivity of my surroundings and I am sure you can feel me swelling with pride at this special place but it does not mean, that I will now pound you with all of the opposite which is the ugliness, despair and negativity that resides in our world BUT I will take you, intermittently, into the TRUTH which is behind the illusion, that is right in front of our eyes, which has been covered up, in plain sight for so long.

It's a LOT of material to absorb and to figure out, with your own mind.

This may sound like a crazy riddle! Like I'm giving you a puzzle to work out! But I promise you, it's nothing like that. It really is crisp and crystal-clear but in a silly disguise.

Now, onto the juicy bits! I will expose the corruption within Governments, our Banking and Political 'systems' and our Courts of Law, as well as divulging the true meaning behind our Birth Certificates that are assigned to each human, which will also unveil the bona-fide reason why we pay taxes into these 'systems'. This will give you the full disclosure of any asset you believe you own, which can range from your Mortgage, Property or Land ownership. Surprisingly, this also includes the State 'Support' Benefits from allowances to pensions, that you may receive from your Government revenue and 'custom houses'.

Over the course of the coming chapters and from start to finish, we, that's me and you, are going to get to know each other a lot better and we may even become friends! But I do feel like starting again from this point, as though we have just met each other.

"Hi there! How are you? I'm happy to meet you."

We can shake hands in a gesture or have a quick hug if you prefer!

Now we can proceed.

Get comfortable wherever you are and allow me to share my awesome adventures and findings that took me down some deep rabbit holes. I know that what I divulge and reveal over the course of these pages will likely make a positive contribution to your life and that is **key** to me, as I assist my fellow humans no matter their gender, race, religion, colour, beliefs, culture, etc.

It's so that we can stand together undivided, with our loved ones, families and our communities in each of our streets, blocks, villages, towns, counties, provinces, states or countries, giving ourselves the freedom to stand together united as a nation, all across the world.

Sadly, we have **all** been dragged through a false set of rules and a misleading narrative from leadership because we were born human and treated as commodities. Simply put, we are being treated as modern day slaves.

>Slavery was never abolished
>
>It was only reconstructed in design

As you read through the pages, you must do what is right for you to do, with all of the information that I provide throughout this book. I am not telling you anything, these are merely my words and my personal experiences about what I have discovered and uncovered. At times you may find that what I share with you, is shocking and disheartening but what is important now, is that *I* know the truth and *you* deserve to know the truth too.

I was led down a path that was previously unknown to me and a hidden world exposed itself, which intrigued me to keep walking along that pathway. I will contribute my explanation with as much detail as I can, so that you can take the time for yourself to research further and delve as deep as you wish to. There may be moments that you may feel like you have fallen down a rabbit hole but that's okay, you will learn what you need to receive during that period and come out of the other end, where you have the option of going in another direction.

No matter what I share with you…it is only **my** truth. Take your time to absorb the information, check in with yourself and see what resonates for you.

Trust your gut instincts.

Listen to your internal wisdom.

Follow your intuition.

Hear your inner-knowing.

It's your personal and private satellite navigation!

You go where you need to go.

Let's go back a few months, to the exact moment when I had the idea of seeing myself as the Mayor of Calgary.

Was it a moment of madness and crazy thoughts?

Or

My gushing pride of the city and its people?

Or

Shall I tell the people of Calgary the truth?

The main reason my thoughts went to the mayorship was so that I could tell the public that the 'systems' in place, have a completely different agenda behind closed doors and that BIG CHANGE is coming NOW, all for the positive of humanity and Earth.

"In the world of minor lunacy, the behaviour of both the utterly rational and the totally insane seems equally odd."
~ *John Kenneth Galbraith - The Affluent Society* ~

2
Mayor Randall Earl Kaiser

"I am worried about our tendency to over invest in things and under invest in people."
~ John Kenneth Galbraith ~

Mmm, let me think.

What is a Mayor?

What is a Mayor for?

What does a Mayor do?

How should a Mayor look?

What should a Mayor believe in?

So many different questions and so many personal opinions!

But ultimately the responsibilities, powers and duties of the Mayor in Council is the political decision-making structure for the City. It is believed that the Mayor has the responsibility for 'policy-making' and translating those policies into actions, delivering processes and proceedings into various municipal services for the Public.

Simply put, the Mayor becomes the Chief Executive Officer (CEO) and represents the Council. The Mayor can recommend bylaws, resolutions and measures which, in his/her opinion, may assist the peace, order, and good government of the municipality.

So, do you think I've got what it takes to be a Mayor?

Could I be the perfect person to become the Mayor of Calgary?

Well, it may be hard to answer that question unless you know anything about me or at least, know that I exist!

Let's start with *why* I believe that *I* would be *great* for this 'role' as Mayor and what I believe a Mayor should be responsible for, when it comes to the people, the community and the greater whole.

It was just another day outdoors, on my daily walk and meeting with the general public and once again I was standing on the peak of Nose Hill Park and as I looked around that 360° gorgeous view, I felt a deep sense of pride. Not just with the magnificent scenery or the location itself but because of the people in the city. This moment filled me with such a mix of emotions and it was not that I personally had achieved anything in particular or possessed something in the city but the people did achieve and possess something!

All of them.

Each and every one of them.

I knew that so many of these wonderful human beings did not realise their greatness in this world.

There is **no-thing** without the people.

It's the **people** who created and designed the architecture.

It's the **people** who built the structures and buildings.

It's the **people** who bring the theatres alive with exuberance.

It's the **people** who bring fun and joy to the parks.

It's the **people** who walk the streets.

It's the **people** who purchase from the shops.

It's the **people** who spend their money.

It's the **people** who bring to life the books in the library.

It's the **people** who live for another day, in hope for a better and easier life.

It's the **people** who keep all the corporations, organizations, businesses and banks going!

YOU are the PEOPLE!

The Government or 'system' never did this – YOU did!

YOU are the Creators of your World that you live in.

I choose not to get into the politics here, of the past behaviours of the 'elite' 'leaders' 'governing bodies' 'monarchies' etc. Directed at any town, province, county or country as I am sure you may have started asking yourself a few questions about this already. You may even have a few statements to throw at me too!

But what I do believe in, is that the people should know how important they are.

The people...that's YOU, need to be congratulated!

If you create something, then the credit is yours.

You are not indebted to anything or anyone from your creation.

The creation is *you*!

YOU are the people bringing everything alive and awakening your towns, cities, villages, regions, areas, counties, provinces and countries, which have the 'ripple effect' touching every area of the whole world. How amazing is that?

You impact the Whole World!

As you contemplate this, let's get back to that moment on Nose Hill and my revelation!

It was January 21st 2021 and it was pretty cold up in those hills. With all of those emotions and my feelings of pride going through me, my thought process was, "If Biden wins this election (in the United States) and the people buy into this bullshit of another New World Order and if he's still in office by September 2021, then I am going to be Mayor of this city!" I put my thoughts into a video, as I regularly do, for my followers and any new friends joining us along the way. If you wish to take a look at this particular video on my YouTube channel – Randall Earl Kaiser – this conversation is titled - *'Calgary Mayor - Not Unless Joe Biden and Kamala Harris make it til September'.*

I returned home and thought no more about it until some days later.

During this time, I had also been considering the idea of returning to some kind of employment, given my situation, but my gut-feeling was to go with my first thought. That was it! No more 'monkey-mind' for me! My brain can only take so much scrutinization or analysis, which can take me around in circles.

Do you ever do that?

Ponder and ponder about something in particular and then come full circle to the first idea that you already had originally.

My heart was telling me the truth which felt good. With that positive notion, I just knew I had to go back to the original consideration of my commitment and promise, which was to put myself as a candidate and nominate me personally, to become the next Mayor of Calgary because that'll make me comfortable. In my mind, the word "comfortable" didn't mean 'cushy' and immersing myself in luxury or in a position of power. That expression of 'comfort' meant that it sat well in my soul, it felt good and it felt right. My intention was to do this duty from a voluntary position and I know full well that any funding for my projects will come directly through my other business connections. So with that in my mind, I knew that I would not need or require a wage, salary or payment from the government.

I was discussing this with one of my friends, Andrea Grace, who owns a business using various alternative healing modalities from hypnosis, Reiki to meditation and positive mind-set. She suggested to me that I could use my conscious mind as a creation tool for my beliefs, which then in turn can create my reality. She encouraged me to imagine what it was that I actually wanted to produce as a Mayor of a City and then proceed to *feel* this feeling and how that would be for me? Then, the next step was to bring that thought alive in my mind visually and to experience the full somatic sensation as a whole and allow the notion to grow and expand. Then channel in a 'counteraction', similar to a weight scale, to offer balance and proportion to the outcome I desired - give to receive - receive to give - no greed or overflow. This sensitive action upon my cells and atoms, would then travel into my subconscious mind to create an outcome that would be supportive to me with my belief system, otherwise, if I didn't do that, it would end up not working out for me in the greater scheme of things.

What a wonderful idea!

My immediate thought was "What if I accept a condo which is paid for by the city, where I have no ownership. I could also have an expense account for food. I don't want to own the condo, just live there whilst I am Mayor." Andrea burst out with excitement, "Now you're thinking! It's all about the balance of giving and receiving. Keep going with that mind-set."

As humans, we have to accept that we *CAN* change things within us, which in turn creates and moves probabilities around us. In our creational processes, we can know, see, feel, sense or visualise the 'end result' we desire and maybe even switch a belief or two to get there!

The concept of not taking payment for my role as Mayor but being fed, watered and having a place to rest, sleep and do my duty, felt good to me! As my intentions feel pure and heartfelt and that's ultimately what I want as an outcome. My realisation that came through this conversation, was a true example and representation of my concept.

Does this make sense to you?

Do you believe that you can create the world you live in?

In my mind, the title of Mayor would be similar to a pastor or a priest. As it was believed, they were 'funded' to 'serve' the people. Well, that's what came to mind for me, that I would be funded with a roof over my head, food and water for nourishment and a place to make space for me, to perform my duty to give the wealth back to the people. Not that I am a pastor or a priest, nor am I a messiah! I'm just Randall, an honest man with a good heart who has God willing to support my intentions, so that I can expose the truth, for the benefit of the masses, not just for the greedy few who only ever produce jaded and shaded outcomes.

BUT remember, the outcome of anything ultimately, is from *your* true intentions that come from within. Think about that!

Some may even utter - "The devil and the angel reside inside of us all."

After having this great chat with Andrea and, later, to myself, the next step was to take a walk downtown and go in the direction of Calgary City Hall. I believed that this was the place to go and register myself for the upcoming mayoral election, in October 2021. When I showed up, I was told that the Elections Official that processes applications would get me started on this trail but I found out, surprisingly, that this process was not managed inside City Hall. This is a million dollar piece of architectural structure that apparently holds the seat of the government for Calgary City Council. So where was everybody? The building's empty! It's a place that's meant to serve as the offices for the Mayor, Councillors and Municipal Clerk and I am being told that I have to travel to the North East part of the city to put in my application! How goofy is that? We have this *huge* and empty building but I am told that I have to travel to another destination which is based outside of the city!? So, I politely arrange an appointment and travel as directed to the North East part of the city via a C-Train.

I do enjoy travelling, especially in comfort, and I know with the C-Train, it's so much nicer than taking those awful buses! How can we be in the 21st century, when it feels like I am sitting on a horse-and-carriage being rattled around in a tin! Did they forget to add shock absorbers and springs? This is another item on my 'List to Change'. I believe that Calgarians have the right to travel in comfort as they pay good money to travel around in this wonderfully expansive city. The corporations should be privileged to have their people using the public transportation system and certainly deserve to be treated accordingly.

When I reached my stop, I still had an additional two-mile walk from the station. I was jiggered to find the building in an obscure little place but I was assured that this structure is still part of city property, how very strange! So, I arrive at the door of my destination, enter the property and go upstairs as directed. I enter a room with my application paperwork ready to hand it over to somebody but due to the insane social-distancing rules, of a system that's gone rogue, there is a woman sitting close to *twenty* feet away from me and she is attempting to converse with me. It was a loud conversation!

>Woman - "Did you bring your deposit and signatures?"

>Me – "No, I need to learn the political process and how I can put myself forward."

>Woman – "Oh, well then, we will have to set up another meeting. You need to go out and get 100 signatures."

>Me – "You mean AUtographs?"

She looked at me strangely.

>Me – "It's the Common Law Jurisdiction. It's our real language."

>Woman – "Well then, you need 100 AUtographs and a deposit of $500."

That was that!

I left the building with new thoughts and ideas and on my way back to my condo in Calgary, I just *knew* that I was ready for this and I was excited to get the necessary AUtographs to put me in the running for Mayor. I was also going to have to tell the people *what* my visions and policies were and *how* I wished to implement this list, as Mayor. I had so many opportunities in my mind and the potential for change, stage-by-stage and step-by-step.

I have a big list!

So, how do I get my 100 AUtographs?

Well, I will continue to share my message with the people that I walk by every day and on my YouTube channels that I have created.

My own channel of course but also a new channel called TAO Eternally. TAO in this case, stands for **T**he **A**Uthentic **O**nes.

Randall in Nature

"The sense of responsibility in the financial community for the community as a whole is not small.
It is nearly nil."
~ John Kenneth Galbraith - The Great Crash of 1929 ~

3
Communication is Key

"A good rule of conversation is never answer a foolish question."
~ John Kenneth Galbraith ~

TAO Eternally came to life when I was chatting with two of my male friends and during our conversation they suggested that I produce a separate channel to create some kind of community. It could be a platform for a variety of people to share similar things but in alternative and diverse ways. What a great idea! Instead of me being a leader and one face, we could have lots of *different* faces.

We decided amongst ourselves that the intention of *TAO Eternally* would be a hub spot for a community of gatherers. With different speakers who could share their wisdom, insights, life experiences, healing and alternative modalities while being energy-raisers, supportive people and/or guides.

Calm the mind. Heal the heart.

We had three men to start with that were myself, William and Lee Mudders and we thought that it would be a great balance to add three women that we knew of. This would harmonise the masculine and the feminine energies. We asked Andrea Grace, Ida Civiero and Danushia Kaczmarek who all happily said 'Yes'. This was the ideal response for me, as our beliefs were similar but different as well, yet we all seemed to meet-in-the-middle. We all had our different angles, ideas and ways of expressing ourselves. How could it not work? So TAO Eternally was born! The first video was uploaded in the latter end of 2020. The group has only reached 106 subscribers presently but I do hope it will expand and grow over time.

"God gave us one mouth and two ears for a goddamn reason!" Stated Jim, who is an old cowboy friend of mine.

Exactly!

There are times we truly need to *listen* to what is being said by another person, more than *talking* to another person. When you listen to someone or something, it offers you the opportunity to experience patience; agreement or disagreement; the ability to resonate or not with the message; empathize; contemplate; experience compassion or humility or some other emotion that the message conveys.

ALL views are welcome because we have so many different beliefs which often depend on our morals, ethics, religious or non-religious truths, health-ideals, perspectives on money and finances, viewpoints on leaders and leadership, educational background, political beliefs, the influence from our own monarchies, views and connections with the cosmos and the universe, our history, our outlooks to the future, literally, everything!

It's a BIG world we live in!

William was asked to host the show and accepted without resistance. I do think he is such a wonderful, gentle man who is curious about life and expresses patience during conversations. You know he is listening with depth and sometimes, he even feels uncomfortable with his vulnerability. As men, we all have this side, whether we choose to get 'in touch' with this part of ourselves or not! Some men see this as a weakness, but I see it as strength! I admire this in other men too as I know what it's like to be an alpha male and using my fists or masculinity without a second thought. I love how now, I can be calm and mindful in my approach as it carries a different kind of strength and power in me and how I relate that to others and them to back me.

Communication is key!

Whatever language people communicate in, we still have our own individual way of interpreting each message we hear. We can hear things hundreds of times without true comprehension but all it takes is a different approach, new words, higher or lower tones or even a softer or curious facial expression and suddenly! ...we can absorb the message. It all becomes clearer in our minds, whether each of us agree or disagree with the explanation given. This then, can create wonder and appreciation of another's belief or life experience and get those 'cogwheels' turning in the brain!

The repetition of words is another form of how we can *re-set* our minds, from a conscious to subconscious level. Tapping into our conscious mind to stimulate the unconscious mind. We all have a mind and a brain as a part of being human. We all have so many layers and this includes early conditioning with various behaviours, morals, beliefs and our own personal thought processes. But over time, as we mature, this evolves and we can re-set, re-programme, re-new and even change our minds.

Open to Closed. Closed to Open.

Objective to Subjective. Subjective to Objective.

I knew that my message of the credit-and-debt 'system' and its *illusions* would be expressed in different ways but we would all have an understanding of the core elements and how we can go through this change in a positive way and thus give guided steps to *how* we can implement the changes into our lives. You have to talk about it to spread the word and its full message because for some, it's not clear and can take some time to understand the concept and for the individual to feel 'safe' and confident to take the necessary steps for change. There is so much hope and wonderment for us all but sadly, many people still experience a sense of hopelessness, currently.

Why do people in general feel hopeless?

Because <u>mankind</u> *manifested* a 'system'.

A 'system' in politics and the banking arena.

The *majority* of people *believed* in this 'system' that was laid before them.

You and me too.

The *majority* of people *trusted* this 'system' put in front of them.

You and me too.

The truth is, most people all over the world are inherently good-hearted. Most people desire an easier and fulfilling way of life but sadly as we have observed, generation after generation after generation, that the public have been locked into a system of *slavery*. This was created to *entrap* families, communities and societies, which was 'drip fed' and enforced upon the people. Which includes the likes of you and me with tools of narcissism, trickery, deception and hidden agendas.

Throughout the centuries, our ancestors often put these *leaders* onto a pedestal out of fear, punishment or the threat of death, if they did not comply and obey the orders. They were continually being beaten down over and over and our ancestors weakened. Not because they were feeble or frail but because there is only so much bullying and abuse you can take as a human soul, before you start to surrender and give over your free-will. Which ultimately relinquishes one's power to the 'system' itself and so the pattern was passed onto each generation and thus repeated with the children and grandchildren and so on.

STOP!

NO MORE!

WE DO NOT CONSENT

WE REJECT YOUR 'SYSTEM'

Thankfully this 'system' is NOW dying.

You can monitor this dying *systemless* 'system', listen closely···   *Beep*

Can you hear it?   *Beep   Beep*

The heart rate is off···   *Beep Beep   Beep*

The pulse is low···   *Beep   Beep   Beep   Beep*

Is this the end-of-the-line···   *Beep   Beep   Beep   Beep   Beep*

Alert! Alert!

The SYSTEM is Malfunctioning!!...   *Beep   Beep   Beep   Beep*

We, the people, are going through the greatest change in history! We are transitioning OUT of this system right NOW. There is no other time but now. Now is all we have.

Some people even call this the Great Awakening!

Some people even think the world has gone mad and it's all topsy-turvy!

But I say, "It was all upside down for a very long time but now we are turning the right way up!" And I know deep in my heart and on behalf of my ancestors before me and my family's future bloodline of my children and my grandchildren, I honour you all! And as long as I have breath in my body, I will never stop loving the people by giving them what they deserve. Which is to know the history of the depth of deception that was hidden from each and every one of you. I will give my *full disclosure* of all the political and banking systems that preferred to make you 'their' slave.

YOU are *not* a slave anymore.

The change is here NOW!

You just have to look all around you, the changes are everywhere in plain sight. But *only* if you choose to *really* look at the changes that are *all* around you.

Does this sound confusing?

Well, here's a recent example of an obvious change that occurred to me, with my communication on my channel.

I believe in the freedom of speech.

And if I'm not mistaken, I believe there is some kinda *legal language* in a sort of *Rights' Bill*, with some written words in a type-of-constitution. This apparently gives us our freedom of speech but I prefer to keep it simple and know that God gave me a voice and a language, so that I could converse and interact with whomever, or whatever, came into contact with me, in the way that I choose to speak.

Do you believe in freedom of speech?

I will not be silenced, limited or banned from opening my mouth and conveying myself in an honest, respectful and open way. However, YouTube took offense to one of my videos and temporarily closed my channel, recently.

Now why would this platform ban my words?

I used clear facts and I merely added my own interpretation to those facts, if they were actually facts.

Why would YouTube ban that?

I was not being violent, aggressive, and abusive or demanding, nor was I taking my shirt off and showing any bits or tits! But according to YouTube guidelines, I was in violation!

YouTube guidelines state, you will not use:
    Spam and deceptive practices
    Fake engagement
    Impersonation
    Links in content
    Spam, deceptive practices and scams
    Sensitive content
    Child safety
    Custom thumbnails

- Nudity and sexual content
- Suicide and self-injury
- Violent or dangerous content
- Harassment and cyber-bullying
- Harmful or dangerous content
- Hate speech
- Violent criminal organizations
- Violent or graphic content
- COVID-19 mis-info policy
- Regulated goods
- Content that features firearms
- Sale of Illegal or Regulated Goods and Services

So which one of my videos defied at least one of their terms and policies?

Oh yes. It was the one where I queried the *cases* and its connection to Covid *deaths* and how the numbers and statistics did not make sense.

Now, all of the information that I shared with my audience was already on the local Governmental websites, with its national statistics for health.

I was only sharing my thoughts and findings because the facts didn't match the numbers but why would the government publish this online to the general public? Alberta apparently had 2500 deaths out of 4.5 million people that was attributed in some way to the *virus*. So, out of complete curiosity I asked "Why are we in a lockdown for an estimated 0.05% death rate?" This was my estimated calculation from the data that I had gathered.

'Lockdown' is actually a term used inside a prison, where the inmates have to return to their cells for an allotted time.

So, when did we become prisoners in my hometown?

I committed no crime! Did you?

Why is there a global pandemic?

I call it a "glow-ball pandemic"! As it's shining the light on the truth.

And why has the world economy been shut down because of it?

I was asking simple questions and I wanted to discuss the details openly, with my followers.

But YouTube said 'no' and banned me from uploading any more videos for seven days.

Now, this type of ban was not applied just against *me,* YouTube has enforced these bans against *ANY* person who has opened the door to any truths, which they do not wish to disclose.

Since March 2020, no matter how many hundreds, thousands or millions of subscribers a YouTube channel has, videos related to *this subject* have been deleted or taken down. Any channel seems to get de-platformed when the content of a video questions the false narrative, even if it was sharing factual truth which is in opposition to the mainstream media's general narrative. To me this was simply stating, "Do not expose us. We are the corporations that you long ago trusted. You must continue to believe our false media and we ORDER you to comply and obey."

This banning was not just applied in Canada and the United States, it was WorldWide!

We're talkin' ALL MainStream Media (MSM). The news, internet, papers, radio, etc.

We, the people, are being silenced. The Truth Givers!

There have been, and still are, mass movements onto other platforms such as Bitchute, Telegram, etc. People are navigating their way around, jumping from one to the other and not really gaining momentum with the real news, views and subscribers. They are being restricted from being able to reach their dedicated followers and supporters from YouTube, Facebook, Twitter and Instagram and all because of algorithms. It has become another form of diversion and separation, so that the 'system', in its present dying phase, would try anything to avoid hearing that *Beep!*

Because of my 'ban', I made a clear decision to play the platform 'game'! I would make them believe that I would comply and obey their rules so as to remain on YouTube and not lose my audience. But I was figuring out how I could agree with them, so that I could also *disagree* with them?

This was easy for me! I can use different words, expressions and images while still giving out the same message. I love words and language so I accept the *game-play* YouTube!

So what's my message and why the heck did I decide to be on YouTube anyways?

It's actually NOT because of Covid-19 or anything I've alluded to up to this point, in this chapter! It's because...

DEBT is an ILLUSION!

There is NO lack of ANYTHING on Earth.

There is ONLY Abundance.

&

Not *ONE* human being should be left out.

I believe that every person on this planet is entitled to comfort and ease and has the right to choose whatever they want, using their own free will.

This is a human right!

What you choose and how you choose to live your life, is just that, *YOUR* choice. But to believe there is not enough of anything on this planet, is a lie.

We Are Unlimited

We Were Limited

by

Global Banking *Systems*

Political *Systems*

Debt –v- Credit

What has this got to do with you?

It's got *everything* to do with You!

Each and every one of You!

Here are some easy questions for you to answer.

Do *you* need water?

Do *you* need food?

Do *you* need shelter?

Do *you* need safety?

Do *you* need clothing?

How do you provide for yourself to receive the above?

Do you work?

Have a job?

Earn a salary?

Get Government assistance?

Are you self-employed at home?

Are you a small business owner?

Are you an international entrepreneur?

Do you have dependencies or receive child or spousal support?

We *all* receive some type of funds or payment to exist. I, you, us and them. We *all* have to use a monetary exchange and accept financial materialism during the course of our lives. This is the world we were born into and it's our world that exists but sadly, a world that we *had* been programmed to live in. The general public have acquiesced to all of the various types of leaders, governing bodies and monarchies that we've grown up with for centuries, whether we consciously chose them or not. We have unconsciously surrendered ourselves to these Political and Banking 'systems'.

BUT at what cost?
To our livelihoods?
To our family?
To our dignity?

Why would these corporations and organizations hurt and harm the very people they are meant to be looking after?

What are we to them?

    A commodity?

A product?

'Them' being the 'elite' or one of the thirteen families that appear to have run the global economy for centuries, which I will go further in depth about in a later chapter, but just know that you, as a human being, are highly valuable to 'them'. Even though you are not looked upon or treated as such. These companies and groups NEED YOU! Did you know that?

'They' are NO-THING without YOU!

They hoard the Gold, silver, platinum and/or other precious metals furtively and craftily so the people of the planet have no access to the trove that actually belongs to Earth. These circles of mobs and groups rule over the stock markets by crashing and expanding business deals with the press of a button. The bands and bodies have created mass global corporations similar to Amazon, Costco, Walmart and Apple. The clubs and clans have created great business ventures like Vodafone, Microsoft, Shell, Honda, Fiat and Mitsubishi.

- o Financials
- o Retail
- o Healthcare
- o Commodities
- o Electronics
- o Oil & Gas
- o Insurance
- o Construction

- Technology
- Space

Everywhere you look, these incredulous people have so much richness, revenue and possessions, that they do not use the general banks as we do. They have such incredible wealth that they move their money around the world via planes, ships, cargo and other various means of exporting or importing their fortune, to a chosen destination.

Why would they do that?

Because they do not wish to disclose the billions and billions and billions of dollars, pounds and other currencies connected to their tonnes of Gold!

The Gold of the People.

The People's Gold.

Your Gold.

That is why they make full use of the underground facilities like bunkers, tunnels and caves to hoard their assets with ancestral artefacts and other treasures - this is all part of THAT world.

"How do *you* know this, Randall?"

Because I have seen this reality and I have been told about it and shown some of the hidden treasures, from the very people that we call the 'elite'. Yes, I have conversed with many influential people as I will further disclose throughout the book and there are a *few* that know of these secrets but *they* choose not to divulge this openly to the public, for various reasons.

The 'elite' are not just a handful of persons, there are millions of them all throughout many countries and continents across the world.

Some are silent.

Some are wild.

Some are whistle-blowers.

Some are nasty.

Some are good.

How can they be good, Randall?

Because there *are* many good people amongst the 'elite' and higher echelons, which may surprise you! I will offer you an example, so that you can wrap your head around this better.

One of the most well-known people around the world was and still is, Princess Diana who married into the British monarchy. Her legacy ensues because of her children, William and Harry. Some people still like to remember her as Lady Diana or the Queen of Hearts! She was a sweet and innocent soul and her family's name was Spencer. If you look through history, it appears that she had been groomed since childhood to marry Charles, the Prince of Wales who is the apparent heir to the British throne as the eldest son of Queen Elizabeth II. Unbeknownst to Diana, there was a 'plan' already underway. Some call this an arranged marriage because of the bloodline that is required for a hidden agenda.

I will leave you with that detail but can you see how she was ultimately a good person with a good heart and tried to use all efforts, against the Monarchy, for the good of the people? She showed deep compassion and was transparent with her connection to humanity.

Now, what did Diana actually discover behind those gilded regal doors?

What secrets were buried so deep that Diana unearthed?

How much did Diana really know of the undisclosed truth?

Maybe this could be another reason for her heartfelt ways with the public, when this woman showed such love and kindness amidst her Royal duties.

Only you can decide and conclude your thoughts about Diana's life and death but it is still, to this day....a mystery. Or is it?

This was why I set up my original YouTube channel back in 2019. Not because of a princess, but for the sake of advertising and broadcasting my news! I had learned so much about the banking 'system' that was so complex for others to get their brain into gear with, as it was mainly mind boggling jargon! But with my absorbable mind, analysis of data and deep curiosity, I figured it out!

I was amazed to find out that when I met with bankers and brokers, most of them didn't know this information!

They would generally resond to me "How do you know about this?" and "I don't know!" not to mention, "You're not a banker/broker." or "You don't know what you are on about!"

"Well, isn't it obvious?" I would say back to them.

Some of them ignored me, some of them thought I was crazy but some of them actually, directly told me the truth!

I was coming from the angle of the 'bigger picture perspective' and I would say to them, "Are you telling me, that a simple bank-to-bank "message" in the form of an MT103 credit-enhancement, stand-alone instrument, with the AUthorized AUtograph of *two* bankers in AGreement, across international boundaries, is the way credit lines are created?"

As you read this question, do you understand what I'm asking?

Basically, it's a business exchange that wishes to engage in a credit enhancement by providing reassurance to a lender that it will honour its obligation by repayment. I wanted to know more, so I would also ask "What's behind that, other than the AUtograph (i.e. signature)?" (I use the term AUtograph for signature, which I shall explain further down the line. Stick with me on this! I will explain this in much more detail in 'Chapter 9 - *Ownership of the People*' and I will tell you why I highlight or capitalise on letters such as AUtograph.)

Your mind will be full of clarity by the end of the book.

I do suggest you take it step-by-step for it all to sink in and to also compartmentalize the data....there is much more information to absorb!

At the very start of my appearance on YouTube, it was more fun and joking around and I even sang a few times! But my passion to share my true understanding of the Political and Banking 'systems' was *always* key in each video. There were times I got sucked into a negative mode, by saying things like "You fuckers!" or "Those Rothschild & Bilderberg families and the Nazis that remained that never left us alone!" But I always came back to my centre and got past the 'blame game' and continued with *how* I wished to create in this world to help others, with my noesis and intelligence.

Creation Rather than Destruction.

If we turn our anger, frustration, disgust and any other horrible feeling inwards, we'll find that it affects our mind, emotions and ultimately, our health in a destructive way. A positive approach would be to set up some type of boundary that works for you. A personal boundary protects oneself. This is giving yourself a clear and distinct line between what behaviour you will accept from others and what behaviour you will not accept from others. When you lower your boundaries, which is simply your personal space, you open the door for others to determine your feelings, thoughts and needs. This is where you get a deeper relationship with yourself, which is not one of those crazy ideas of mine but it's another part of being healthy. When you take responsibility for yourself, it's so empowering! For example: when you know that something doesn't *feel* right, well that's just it...you *know* it's not right and this gives you the free-will to reject it. It really is that simple but it does take time to become a master of this skill. The mastery is confidence, trust and believing in your own identity as the human that you are.

At some point down the line, finding peace is to for-give and yes, this means all those atrocities that were done to you and your loved ones.

Take your time with this notion and be kind to yourself as you have been through a lot!

It may even take layers of for-giveness and it has to be done in your own way and in your own time. I separate the word forgiveness to for-giveness because it's a word that carries so many meanings but I believe that forgiveness is not *accepting* behaviour or *condoning* behaviour or even forgetting the behaviour of the 'system' - but when you for-give, you give-for.

You give for to You.

You give the Love to You, not the Love to the 'system'.

You deserve to give You the Love.

Our emotions can get 'triggered' by the TRUTH and we can *react* very quickly, which generally brings us down. Then we are left with all of those yucky feelings swimming around inside of us and even attracting physical pain. These are moments in time and an opportunity for us to examine what we are really feeling and be completely honest with ourselves, so that we can change those 'triggers' and reactions.

It's a moment to moment thing and you have all the time in the world!

It's better to find peace in oneself, rather than taking a flaming torch and a pickaxe to chase or hunt down the very people who may have triggered us, for personal vengeance or retribution! Justice will prevail with good leaders.

Some things also have to be left for justice, to the higher realms to deal with. Whether you call it Karma, God or something else, you know that there is truth somewhere in that.

The 'systems' that were put in place decades and decades ago, were installed to *protect* the 'elite' and keep their structures alive and well. However, those structures are now collapsing before our very eyes. The 'system' is failing and the 'elite' have nowhere else to run or hide. *They* are no longer in the position to take anything more from the people. You can see it unfolding daily. We are *already* transitioning into a new 'system' that *'gives to'* the people, rather than *'takes from'* the people. Some call this system the Quantum Financial System (QFS) - which will be a United States central controlled **GOLD-backed** system, replacing the United States central controlled **swift** 'system'.

Some call this system - GESARA and NESARA, which are acronyms;

GESARA = Global Economic Security And Reformation Act.
NESARA = National Economic Security And Reformation Act.

These 'Acts' have been written and refined by great minds of the twentieth and twenty-first centuries in order to reset planet earth and humanity on a sustainable governance foundation.

I personally prefer referring to this new system as 'Quantum Conscious Banking' (QCB).

The full details are yet to be disclosed, at the time of me writing this book but it is believed to be a system, which can never be misused, abused or tampered with again.

Now, I know what you are going to ask me after reading that part.

"If we have had a 'system' mislead and deceive us, how can we be sure that it will not happen again?

Who are the new governors?

Who do we trust now?"

Patience.

All will be revealed over time and the very few that are in the know, keep these details close to themselves.

Why?

Because there is *still* a **war** going on as I convey my words to paper and *we are winning*! A war in many ways, in so many formats, everywhere.   No one can escape it.

I am not here to create fear in your world but to present you with clear information because when you have clarity, then you have free choice. An honest, reasonable and straightforward choice for yourself, loved ones, friends, neighbours, colleagues and strangers that come and go in your life. This enables you to decide your lifestyle, health, education, financial and leisure choices. When you feel at peace, you can focus and make wise decisions and thus in turn, learn from unwise judgements and unfavourable outcomes.

I have had some great conversations over many years and some of them have made such an impact on me whether it was about the metaphysical, the spiritual realm or around the dimensional land we reside on. I now have some very special friends and contacts from around the world and for this, I am truly grateful.

One of my 'brothers in arms' along this journey and who I have known for a number of years, is Sacha Stone. He kindly shared one of my videos back in 2020, where I was talking about the Federal Reserve, the Treasury and U.S. President Donald J. Trump. I wanted to show the people that we are moving beautifully into a **Re-Public** which has no corporate agenda and has a completely different meaning than the political party, named as the *Republic-an* Party. Surprisingly to me, the numbers jumped up on my views and I had additional followers and people were even asking me for interviews to put up on their personal channels. They wished to share my messages. Of course I said "Yes!" to these requests.

Once again I say thank you to:

Jennie Byers

Leah Mattinson

Andrea Grace

Danushia Kaczmarek

Benjamin Mensah

Hamid & Nadea

Aida Farhat

Roman Light

And a few others that I have forgotten the names of! ...but I still send my thanks to you through the airwaves.

I resonated with so many characters and the range of conversations was diverse. I even got the opportunity to be in conversations surrounding a gentleman named Gregory Hallet. For those of you who don't know who he is, this man feels that he has an official claim to the British throne, as King John III. He also claims that Queen Elizabeth II is a fraud!

I personally do not believe in these types of chosen leaders, especially when you realise the true reason *why* they exist or how they came to be *elected* above the people. All of these appointed 'leaders' were simply because of greed and the need for control and power. Nonetheless, Gregory's story is *very* intriguing and it does get you to question the facts and the fiction.

It can be so educational to look into history with so many books and television documentaries discussing theories on monarchies, which are not just in the alternative media but everywhere, exposing the royal bloodlines. The British Broadcasting *Corporation* (BBC) is one of the national broadcasters of the United Kingdom, there is a particular documentary that shares with the British public that they have discovered their own Queen of England is not the true heir and the throne is waiting for a man in Australia to take his seat!

The 'system' is blatantly exposing the truth to the people of Great Britain and they turn a blind eye!

This is another example of how the TRUTH is staring you right in the face. The illusion is always there for you to see, it's just what you *do* with that truth. Again, it comes to boundaries and what you will accept and what you will not accept.

To date, that Aussie guy declined the position! Brilliant! Would you take the throne as King or Queen if you were given that kind of opportunity? You can watch that documentary online titled *'The Truth about Elizabeth II'*, narrated by Tony Robbins.

Now, I am jumping to an opposite but relevant theme here.

Have you heard of Atlantis and/or Lemuria?

Another person I met in 2020 was Huna Flash who captured me with his native history of elders and ancestry, which all dated back to the Lemurian language. The age of space in our past, has its original magnetic Ley Line grids across the Earth and he teaches his wisdom and how we will embrace the future times to come, on the Earth.

I love speaking to people and listening to their experiences, you can learn so much! It sounds opposite but as it's connected to the Earth, then this affects all life and everything living which is *you*! That's why it's relevant.

 If you were to get to know me, you'd discover that I have an open attitude towards these new areas of information *even if it blows my mind!* I see it as a way to open and expand myself. I believe if these people have enough conviction in their hearts to have the courage to come forward in the public arena and talk authentically about their own lives, then why shouldn't I support them? I am but the observer and can choose to believe, reject or see life in any way I see fit - regardless how radical or 'straight-laced' it may be! We are shifting and evolving constantly, yet, it's only a brief moment in time that I get to share with someone. In each moment we have, we get the freedom to *choose* anything we wish to be responsible for, in our lives.

You get a lot to offer, in a short amount of time on both of my video channels. Again those channels are 'Randall Earl Kaiser' and 'TAO Eternally' on YouTube. All viewers will get links to all the other wonderful people that I have met along the way.

All for FREE.

In Service to All

We are the Truth Givers!

Next, I go back a few years to when I travelled over the seas and left a huge suitcase with Rodrigo Roa Duterte, the current President of the Philippines.

"All of the great leaders have had one characteristic in common: It was the willingness to confront unequivocally the major anxiety of their people in their time. This, and not much else, is the essence of leadership."

~ John Kenneth Galbraith ~

4
Victory Notes

"The process by which money is created is so simple that the mind is repelled."
~ John Kenneth Galbraith - Money: Whence It Came ~

I got to understand the Legal System alongside Common Law Jurisdiction, with my entry into the courthouse scene some years back, concerning a property that I owned. From that point on, I steered down a pathway which led me onto a variety of serendipitous scenarios and connections. It was a slow process over many years but one of those 'links' in the chain of events was with a Filipino man who lives in Vancouver, named Angelito Mallonga. I listened to his story and met with him many times at his home. He would share with me clear information and paperwork that was linked to the massive amounts of Gold that were verified by bank deposit certificates from his predecessors, as well as deposits of 'Victory notes'.

What are Victory notes?

Victory notes was an exchange of currency to the Philippines during WWII, these notes were printed in 1944 in the U.S. BUREAU of Engraving and Printing- the last Philippine currency printed by the United States. Replacement notes are indicated by a star prefix to the serial number. General MacArthur brought with him this new currency when he landed on Leyte Island, Philippines.

So, with my understanding, this means that the Gold is left where it is but here is some medium of exchange to play with! Meaning credit, so thank you very much! But this is where the story unfolds and I certainly would recommend taking some time to research further.

The Victory note was taken out of circulation but a lot of the notes were deposited.

But by whom?

And where is the money or the Gold?

Now, President Ferdinand Marcos created a lot of these notes, funds and his renowned 'Marcos accounts' during his term as the 10th President of the Philippines, 1965-1986. During his time in office, his decisions were made to leave the Gold in its residency and any occupational destinations, in underground bunkers, tunnels, caverns and caves. It was believed that they would start a process of bringing this back to the banks, through safekeeping receipts and an *assay* of measurement of the volume of Gold.

How is this done?

Well, the naked eye is unable to determine the purity of metals and this can hold true for ore and jewellery alike but in order to determine the percentage of composition of a sample of Gold, the sample must be *assayed*. Gold can be assayed in one of three ways:

1. Fire - at high temperatures. Using reactants to create the flux.
2. Aqua Regia - a specific combination of hydrochloric and nitric acid.
3. ED-XRF Spectrometry - a type of energy dispersive with X-ray fluorescence.

Now you know how to assay your Gold, let us get back to the Marcos accounts.

My story is a long one so I will condense this into simpler terms.

As I mentioned earlier in this chapter, I had met and was working with Angelito Mallonga from Vancouver. Angelito is also known as ArchAngel Mallonga but I will call him *Angel* for the rest of this book. He is a highly educated engineer from the Philippines with a Spanish background. He was chosen by the family of Jose Bautista Cruz, to be the Special Irrevocable Power of Attorney, when Jose died.

EDSA Revolution

Jose Bautista Cruz was a great friend of President Ferdinand Marcos. Jose is also part of 'EDSA Revolution' and is also known as the 'People Power Revolution' as the demonstrations during the month of February 1986, made news headlines, as "The revolution that surprised the world."

Angel's lifelong friend, General Carlos Malana and supporter of the Cruzen Philippine Fund process, was a hero during the EDSA Revolution as he physically demanded that Martial Law back down, after the people revolted against the Martial Law regime which was now directed by the frightened and soon-to-be exiled, President Ferdinand Marcos. I met with General Malana in Manila on more than one occasion, which I will expand upon in the following two chapters.

The documents that Angel had shared with me, clearly showed that he has the power of representation of that account. This was ONE of many, "Off-ledger" accounts. There are hundreds if not thousands of accounts just like this one, around the world backed by ancient Gold which can also be called *collateral accounts* of heritage funds. Angel proved his paperwork to me and I started to question everything that I once knew to be true.

There is an official document that I have added at the end of this chapter generated by the Board of Governors of the Federal Reserve System which was devised in the Office of the U.S. Treasury, on the 11th of August 1979. It begins…

"That I, Jose Bautista Cruz coded Cruzen Philippines, legal age, depositor in trust of Tiburcio Villamor Marcos, legal heir of Queen Enimecia Cruz Villamor-Marcos, Her Majesty Queen of Spain, Owner of El

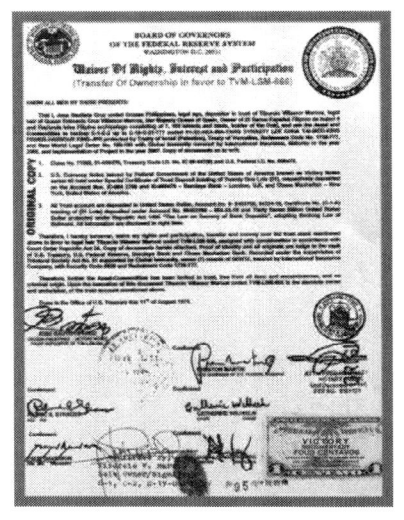

Transfer of Ownership

Banco Espanol Filipino de Isabel II and Hacienda Islas Filipina archipelago consisting of 7,169 islands and Islets, holder of the Gold, and use the Asset and Commodities to backup······"

The historical links with humble beginnings from Spain to Indonesia are worth looking into but I will share some simplicity for you here.

The *Peso* ₱, which translates to "weight" by virtue of its origins from Spain, became a monetary unit which was issued through paper banknotes, which began its circulation during the period of 1851/2 for the Philippines. Prior to this fractal currency, they used locally-produced, crude copper from local mines, as well as bronze coins, silver and Gold. The history, over hundreds of years, is so interesting to delve into but I will keep focused on my story which leads onto the money trail of the Marcos Billions and the Philippine Government, which affects the *current* economy of the people in the Philippines.

Since WWII, these Victory notes were placed into a confidential identity or person and not into a government's name.

Victory Notes

As you can imagine, with the amount of information arriving in all directions around me, which was exposing the banking world, Gold, money, deposits, etc, I needed to know more, so I thought the best place to go and ask some questions was the Federal Reserve or the U.S. Treasury or anyone who had ever worked there. So, I contacted the office of Paul Volcker.

"Paul Adolph Volcker Jr. was an American economist. He was Chairman of the Federal Reserve under U.S. presidents Jimmy Carter and Ronald Reagan from August 1979 to August 1987. He is widely credited with having ended the high levels of inflation seen in the United States during the 1970s and early 1980s. He was the chairman of the Economic Recovery Advisory Board under President Barack Obama from February 2009 until January 2011."

Paul Volcker began a *Think Tank* back in 2015/6 using this scheme, to try and figure out how to gain the trust of the people, through its government.

Think Tank is made possible by generous support from the Smith Richardson Foundation, the Bernard and Irene Schwartz Foundation, the Lynde and Harry Bradley Foundation, the John M. Olin Foundation, the Donner Canadian Foundation, the Dodge Jones Foundation, and Pfizer, Inc.

I reached out to various people at *Think Tank* and tried to communicate my findings about these ancient funds, but not *one* person would converse with me.

I did manage to contact a man named Richard Dohner, who is a Chief Economist at the U.S. Treasury.

I actually got to speak to him over the telephone. During our first conversation, he was polite and kind in his manner, after I shared some of my collected information. He did say to me "Well, you don't need to pay attention to that stuff, it's all good. We have our monetary system in place."

What he was implying was the Banking 'system' that is backed by **our** credit creation, signed with **our** AUtographs versus any asset-backed monetary system. The chat continued:

> Richard: "You sound like a good guy Randall, with some monetary intelligence."
>
> Me: "Would you mind if I shared some of this stuff with you via email and then maybe we can talk again?"
>
> Richard: "Sure, that's fine, I have time for that. You're a nice guy."

Well, I do have that type of approach with other people, where they can find it challenging to get rid of me!

The second conversation...some weeks later:

> Richard: "Hi Randall, good to talk to you again."
>
> Me: "Have you taken a look at my emails yet?"

Richard: "No, sorry. I haven't had the time yet."

We continued with pleasantries and general talk and simply played a 'nice' game together. Richard ended the phone call with "I'll take a look, call me again."

Our third and final exchange...some weeks later:

Me: "Hello Richard, how are you doing?"

Richard: "I have nothing to comment on and we are going to have to leave it at that."

Me: "Yes but we had a nice chat last time we spoke."

Richard: "I have nothing to comment on and we are going to have to leave it at that."

Me: "Is everything okay? I thought we had got on well and you were going to read my emails."

Richard: "I have nothing to comment on and we are going to have to leave it at that."

Me: "Yes, I can hear that Richard."

That was the end of that!

Did that intrigue me?

Fuck yeah!

I was thinking "You've got something here buddy!

That paperwork was *no* copy that I had sent over to him and it must mean something. Something that is hidden or fraudulent."

This led me onto my two trips to Indonesia.

But for the next chapter, I will begin with the very first excursion to Jakarta because I feel you need to know first, *why* and *how* it all links up to the money and the Gold!

"One of the greatest pieces of economic wisdom is to know what you do not know."
~ John Kenneth Galbraith ~

5
Filipina 'Gold'en Girls

"But there is merit even in the mentally retarded legislator. He asks the questions that everyone is afraid to ask for fear of seeming simple."
~ John Kenneth Galbraith - The Age of Uncertainty ~

The first time that I realised that I, Randall Kaiser, had the potential of getting myself involved in a humanitarian project, which could expand to throughout the worldwide, it felt pretty good indeed! It felt *right* in my soul.

As I continued to dig deeper into these 'systems', I respected the fact that I was thinking of *'them'* in a hierarchical manner, in other words, *'they'* owned the accounts and somehow *'they'* owned that position.

But this was when I also realised, that ANY-THING that BIG is NOT *'owned'* by *one* man or *one* woman, family or nation⋯it's owned by GOD!

So, with that idea in my mind, I pulled myself out of the illusion of 'owner-ship' into the world of 'service' to ALL, which includes humans, animals, all life and matter. This actual timeline of events is covered in these coming chapters and how that information was *jarred* into me, which began on a night flight to Manila.

I was staying in a hotel based in Quezon City, which is a part of Manila, which is highly urbanized and the most populated city in the Philippines. I was accompanied by Margaret Kocsis during my trip. She was my aid on this venture, offering me support and funding. I think of her as family, not just as a friend and I am so grateful for our connection.

The morning after we had arrived, I decided to go out for a walk on my own and see what wonders I could find out in the street. I left the Hotel and took a look around me and then looked back towards the Hotel. There was this little girl there. She was sitting on a piece of cardboard on the concrete, where she had obviously been sleeping for the night. This sweet soul was about 6/7 years of age and the dress she wore was ragged, her hair matted and her skin filthy. She stood up and asked me for some money as I was close to her. I was surprised by my immediate reaction, as I sat by her on the sidewalk and just wept in front of her, at the heart wrenching sadness of the situation that I was in the midst of experiencing. I never thought I would have ever reacted this way, being a strong male but in my mind, and as the tears flowed, I was saying to myself "Fuck, I've got to do something about this!" So, with that, I pulled out a few pesos that I had in my pocket and gave it to her. The amount I gave could have equated to a few weeks of begging in the streets. And yes, I could also see the bigger picture; that she could be a trap; an actress used by her guardians or family to extricate money from people like me and then throw this child back to the streets, with little regard for her innocence but to continue her 'role' that she probably never chose.

It was a fleeting moment in time but the experience certainly impacted me and when I returned to my hotel room, I chose to move on from this sad situation so that I could continue with the day ahead of me and execute my plans of action.

When Margaret and I left the hotel, I ensured that I brought along my *huge* suitcase that was filled with gifts, documents and paperwork that I would offer to people along the way. Some may call this a bribe, but I call it offering gifts! I knew this could open doors for me, to reach my goal of meeting the man himself, Rodrigo Duterte, who is the 16th and current President of the Philippines. Duterte also served as the Mayor of Davao City for 22 years.

We spent days travelling around and I was beginning to get frustrated because I wanted to get right in front of the President. I knew he was not in Manila but over in Davao City. I knew of this because of my connection with 'Queen Legaspi' and some others know of her as 'Queen Majesty'. She is a self-proclaimed and highly followed *idol* in the Philippines and I do have respect for her, even though I may not agree with some of her expressions in life. During a meeting, I knew she was going to meet Duterte and I piped up "I'm coming along with you!" The response from General Carlos Malana and those who were currently travelling with us, piped up "No you're not. You will get into trouble." I looked straight towards Margaret and said "Do you wanna go?" And without any hesitation, she said "Yes!" We both knew that the General and Angel were pissed off with our decision but I told them "We are not making any headway here and I'm not gonna pussyfoot around anymore. That suitcase is gonna get delivered to Duterte, come hell or high water!"

So, we hopped onto a plane going towards the north end of Mindanao Island, where we were picked up in a Volkswagen Beetle. "Where the hell are we going to put our gear?" I asked. Their response was "I don't know, we never thought of that." So, with an eye roll and a deep intake of breath, I waved over a taxi cab and as the driver pulled up I said to him "We need to follow those guys in that car." This taxi-man looked at me, at the *Beetle* and the men who came along with it, that I can only describe as a similarity to a Rastafarian style, who were waiting for us to get in the car.

Taxi: "I am not following them! Those people are Muslims and you will get into trouble!"

I was getting impatient but I kept my cool with this guy and I told him "Buddy, just follow from a distance, you don't have to get involved. Just tag behind them, as they are taking me and my friends where we need to go." Naturally, I offered extra bucks and thankfully he agreed and we were on our way.

We continued northwest, heading towards Davao City from Iligan City and we stopped to rest during the day, as the crew felt it would be best for me to travel during the night. As parts of the country were raw and real and what I would call 'uncivilized', just imagine the Wild West, in times gone by. This was because of their native ways.

I was cautioned with various fears of me being kidnapped or attacked because I was the tall 'white' guy. In one way I agreed with them, to reassure them and their beliefs but I also opposed their fears with confidence "We won't be attacked." I truly felt okay with this as I did not fall into their worries or fears as we passed along our journey. Happily, we travelled when the sun had gone down.

There were five of us in total that filled up the taxi vehicle. We had the driver and myself in the front passenger seat, while in the back, sat Margaret, Queen Legaspi and one of her security guards.

During one of those twilight nights, the cab driver was doing his job and the other three people in the back of the car were sleeping. I could feel myself nodding off but I kept waking myself up, as I wanted to see the countryside and the lands with the limited view of light. As we were getting closer to the City, I was observing the driver as I could see that he was beginning to tire and fade and I said to him "Are you okay? I can drive if you want to rest up." "No, I'm good to keep going," he replied. But something inside of me felt to keep alert, awake, eyes wide open and watch on. Within minutes, the driver fell asleep at the wheel and we were heading towards another car for a direct hit! My instinct kicked in and I reached forward and grabbed the steering wheel, thanks to my long arms and body length! With an additional body slam to the driver, I managed to steer the car back onto the right side of the road where he then slammed on the brakes and we came to an abrupt stop, with everyone jolting forwards and going into a sudden state of shock.

"You are an *angel*! You saved the Queen of the Philippines! We could have been killed or badly injured. Thank you! Thank you!" Proclaimed Queen Legaspi. Wiping the sweat off my forehead, I say to them "Okay, that's fine but I am driving from now on towards our destination, so you buddy! Move outta the driver's seat." With that, I drove the rest of the way into the City but it was not all smooth sailing, as I did not really understand the road signs and at one point I went the wrong way down a one way street!

> Team: "Oh my God, do you want us to be arrested?!" The team yelled at me.

> Me: "They drive like this all over the place!"

> Team: "Not in Davao City! There are rules here we must obey. It's the safest place in the world for a reason. The Police are all over you the minute you go off the rules. Marshall Law is big here."

> Me: "Okay, okay, I will follow your rules, just help me out with the signs."

Further on we pulled into the nearest 'Jollibee' which is similar to a McDonalds drive thru. After we had a full breakfast, the driver felt awake and rejuvenated enough to continue the journey and resumed his role in the driver's seat.

Because of the people in the car, we knew where Duterte's home or 'safe place' was. We had a predetermined plan for the location which we knew was down a side street. We also knew that we would have to go through various checkpoints and stops, where the guards would ask for our identification and paperwork to declare who we were.

Things were taking a lot longer than anticipated and we pulled over to the side of the road, as we were figuring out what we should do. But I was beginning to get tired and my dissatisfaction started to creep in, as I felt we were now stalling the situation. The weather was so hot and I was starting to get overheated sitting in the car, trying to come to some decision of any action we should take. As my sweat was beginning to pour out from me, I suddenly jumped out of the car and grabbed the suitcase "Which way? Come on you guys, we don't have all fucking day!"

We walked along and reached the first checkpoint. Thankfully, the rifles were put down as I approached them with my open heart, a big smile and not forgetting my cowboy hat, which usually softens situations as people don't normally see someone wearing one of those walking down a street in Davao City! I said to them "We got some stuff for the President!" As I showed them my suitcase. They opened it up and moved us onto the next checkpoint. Each time it was the same scenario, until we met with 'Minnie Rose' who was the Head of Security for that area. She was sweet and said "Bring that suitcase over here. We are going to have to look through it."

Me: "Sure thing." As they filtered their way through it.

Minnie Rose: "You know he's not here, Duterte."

Me: "Oh my God!"

Minnie Rose: "You can't meet with the President that easily!"

Me: "Well, what's the next step?"

Minnie Rose: "You can take your picture over there." As she pointed to a life-size cardboard *cut-out* of him! So Margaret and I did just that, took our picture with the illusion of Duterte!

Minnie Rose: "You can go to Bong Go's Headquarters."

This is Duterte's right hand man who also loves photobombing any images taken on their official trips!

We were given the directions and followed the instructions. When we arrived, the guardsmen marched towards us and I said "Hello, Minnie Rose told us to turn up here, she gave us the directions to take." Thankfully, they understood my English, lowered their guns and led us inside and to our surprise, there was Minnie Rose! She accepted the gifts from my suitcase, on behalf of the President and the paperwork was administered.

Wow! What an accomplishment, I was thrilled!

But I was not giving up on this one! We still had high hopes to have that meeting with Duterte and we would continue to do our best, to get an appointment with him. Another option was for us to go to the Mayor's Office to connect with the Presidents' daughter Sara, who is the Mayor of Davao City. I was even more determined than ever to come back again, as I knew this was *not* over. I had not gotten this far, for it to grind to a halt. My intention for the next visit was to solidify the fact that he had received and acknowledged that paperwork that I handed over, from my suitcase of goodies and I wanted to know what he had to say about it.

Land Bank Official and Councillor in Davao City

Central Bank of the Philippines

The 'Gold'en delight was not always the material kind, as etched in my memory, it was another young girl whom I met. I was walking along in the drizzling rain when out of nowhere, I spotted a child aged about 7/8 years and she approached me "Sir, Sir! Would you like to buy my umbrella?" It was a cheap canopy but her smile was big and wide, which made me smile back at her. I thought I would play along with this smiling capitalist!

Me: "Does it look like I'm made out of sugar?"

Girl: "What do you mean?"

Me: "Do you think I'm going to melt in this little bit of rain?"

The girl pouted her lips and pulled her face into a sad look, displeased at my response.

Me: "I like your style!"

Girl: "What do you mean?"

Me: "Well, you've got a nice smile and you're rocking with your business. I'm in the banking world and I will give you a loan of money but it's a gift from God and you don't need to pay me back."

It was plain to see from her facial expression, that she got the bit about God but not the banking terms but she smiled anyway. So, I gave her $20 which probably was a weeks' wage for her selling her wares.

Me: "You keep that umbrella, it's still yours."

She was so happy at this interaction between us, that she danced along beside me as I continued to walk along the streets, back to my hotel. She was telling me story after story with such animation, exuding her joy and fun. When I arrived at the hotel, I turned to her,

Me: "Okay sweetheart, I gotta go now. Have a good day, it was so much fun!"

I think I even remember a quick hug from her before we parted.

I realised after bumping into these two young, sweet children on my travels, that charity is not the answer. It's the idea of teaching them to fish, rather than giving them the fish. The first girl that I saw lying on the cardboard on the concrete, was too overwhelming and emotional for me but this second girl, well···I was in a different head-space and state of mind, so with that I used a different approach.

I have noticed along this intense journey, that I have to choose to separate my emotions and look at the bigger picture. I feel that I am unable to help humanity and be at my best with a clear and focused plan, if I just fall into a place of deep sadness. Sometimes I can get into the 'warrior' mode where I can take charge and demand for our human rights because of my sympathy, rather than coming from a place of empathy and compassion, which offers different results.

What do I mean by different results?

This is how I see it.

If I am crying at the pain and suffering of the children, it brings a sense of hopelessness and a powerless feeling. Like I cannot help them. But I know this is not true. When I can have clear thoughts in my mind with visions and ideas, creating plans and ideals and what steps do I have to do, to bring these ventures and projects to life. Then situations flow, synchronicities happen and it comes alive! When I am in grief or anger, then I have no clarity and become heavy, weighed down and unsettled. It feels like I come to a full-stop. But when I have clarity, I become light and I feel that I am in my power.

It's a bit similar to my chat with Andrea that I shared with you, when we talked about finding balance of the conscious and subconscious mind and how a person has the ability to bring to life the outcome they desire.

I have plenty of time for tears and to express those emotions when I can get the results, support and aid the people. I will address those feelings and say 'hi' to them. I will welcome them in and then let them ride through me. This is far more positive, as it's a bit like a detox of the emotions, so they move through the body instead of residing in the body. If the emotions are left inside oneself to stagnate, it will show up in your physical body as pain or disease. The mind or emotional state will enhance any doubts, fears, anxieties and then you lose the confidence and trust of your own well-being and free-will. This is why you *must* find the time in your day, to connect to yourself through various methods that support and enhance oneself, so that you can continue giving your service to the world.

You are important, take care of yourself.

The 'Filipina 'Gold'en girls' were two, sweet, innocent children who were such beautiful souls and not designed to 'beg' for a basic life. They both caught my attention in the streets as I was minding my own business and they both reminded me that I was going in the right direction in life, all with God's plan, for me to give my service to humanity.

These children are the Future
These children are Worldwide
These children deserve a Good life
These children need to know the Truth
These children are the Gold

"Under capitalism, man exploits man; while under socialism just the reverse is true."
~ John Kenneth Galbraith - A Life in Our Times ~

6
Jakarta Gems

"Men can labour to make sense out of single steps toward the goal without ever pausing to reflect that the goal itself is ludicrous."
~ John Kenneth Galbraith - The Affluent Society ~

We tried to use the same tactics as before to reach Duterte's home. We also knew that he had a 'safe' office space elsewhere. I must admit that it was one of the most surreal sites that I have ever visited. It looked like some children had built a fort-like playhouse with turrets and various sizes of pieces of wood and sticks, barricading it with tin, metals and a tumbled barbed wire around the top platform. The only way that you knew it was not a playhouse, was because of the armed guards with machine guns, which gave that one away!

I chuckled to myself as I thought "In the Philippines, the population is an estimated 100 million people and this guy is their leader and he is working from an office, that's in a ram shackled fort! The Malacañang Palace is supposed to be the official residence and principal workplace of the President of the Philippines. He's my kinda guy!"

But I was not making any headway, with my original process to get closer to him. And his fort in Davao City only proved to me that the corruption in the dark political side of Manila was real and the 'elite' did not like the style of Rodrigo Roa Duterte.

I made this second trip to Jakarta, Indonesia, mainly due to my conversations and connection with a high-level banker named Eddy. I had been introduced to Eddy during my first visit through synchronistic circumstances, like so many of my meetings. We became good friends. He is a highly knowledgeable man in the banking industry and at that time, Eddy also had the potential of running for Governor of the Central Bank of Indonesia. But because he was aware of the deception and the truth of the 'systems', he chose to be on the 'good' side of the misrepresentation of credit and debt. He had grand visions, plans and humanitarian projects in mind.

Randall with Eddy (middle) and friend

Eddy also brought to my attention the Swissindo. This was the third time that I had heard about this and I wanted to learn more about the details.

What is Swissindo?

The Swissindo is short for 'Swissindo World Trust International Orbit' (WKE-UNS), also known as NEO the United Kingdom of God Sky Earth which is an organisation that claims to "Work towards eliminating the debt of everyone on Earth". NEO does not stand for the guy from the Matrix movies! And the United Kingdom is not the UK of Great Britain. The 'United Kingdom' means the whole world! The Kingdom of God, Uniting the People.

On their website Swissindo.news, their mission states:

"World Kingdom Empire – Swissindo World Trust International Orbit - aims to free humanity from financial and physical burdens of the slavery systems, reconnecting to nature, back to basics and back to Source, creating Spiritual awareness and aligning Heaven back to Earth through Payment Order 1-11 Implementation.

WKE-UNS is a non-profit humanitarian organization that wishes to present to you, a World Solution Gift Offer of Payment Order 1-11 of the Construction of the Universe for the people of the World in 253/357 Countries.

Our mission is to return the world's freedom and inheritance back to the people, to every man, woman and child in this world."

Another statement - "It is by Divine Authority of the Creator that all People are endowed with certain unalienable, natural Rights and Liberties; which no authority, man-made law, government or religion can rightfully diminish or abolish. Any power that attempts to do so is tyrannical and illegitimate, even if it operates according to its own laws – for such tyranny is a denial of the Natural Laws of Creation."

The Swissindo headquarters are based in West Java, Indonesia, and is led by the sovereign, Sino Soegihartonotonegoro. His full title is

'HM.Mr.Sino.AS IR.S"2".SOEGIHARTONOTONEGORO.HW.MA.ST.M1 (Royal K.681 M1)'. He is known as 'M1'! But from this point onwards, I will name him 'Sino'.

Sino ('M1')

The first time the Swissindo came to my attention, was through my good friend, Sacha Stone who also shared his story about the Royal families that he had met with. The second time I heard about it was via Neil Keenan who shares his talks about the Indonesian Collateral Accounts and how he has had a 12+ year struggle against the Cabal. During this time, he has learned how the 'elite' operate, who they are, what they are planning and why they are doing it.

So, when Eddy shared his story with me about the Swissindo, I showed him my papers that I had brought along with me from Canada. These papers were from an Indigenous group that were trying to bring these 'credit instruments' into the banking system as a land claim. The ancient people had so much gold underneath the land that it's not even funny! It's completely true and a common native story often found in a land claim.

Here is what a standalone credit instrument is:

➢ Credit = AUthorisation * recognition * approval.

- ➢ Instrument = legal * official * written.

- ➢ Credit instrument = bank note * cheque * bond * letter.

- ➢ Credit instrument = guarantees payment of a specific amount to a specific person.

So, at that time, we felt we should bring these papers along with us, as proof for the people, we were meant to meet along the way.

These papers belonged to a dear friend of mine, Capilano, who passed away near the end of April 2021. He also had a land claim that was never disputed by the Government of Canada nor had any backing from nations around the world.

Margaret and I had the pleasure of Eddy's company during our trip through Indonesia where he introduced me to Henry. Henry had a similar story to Sino but he and his team were not affiliated with the Swissindo. They were aware of each other but were not collaborating together as a unit.

Henry invited us to his home in Depok City and I do believe that he has a large following of intelligent banking people. Yes, I think that I can put myself on that pedestal of 'cognition of intelligency'! And I will pop Margaret up there on that podium too!

During our lengthy meeting, he questioned us both on our knowledge of the banking industry. We also shared our humanitarian visions, ideals and projects. Before our meeting came to an end, Henry offered me and

Margaret a 50 million dollar 'bond' for our projects! Henry signs his name with two Autographs, one as the Banker and the one as the Sovereign living man. The bond was then stamped and sealed. He gave us the pen that he had held for his AUtographs on the bond, to use as evidence and for any required forensic proof of his fingerprints. He knew the processes for a standalone credit instrument.

Henry and Eddy are under the title of the Collateral House of the Gold & Treasure. The Gold remains in one location and the physical Bond is created for credit, usually through a Bank or a Banking system.

Henry has the AUthority, as the right hand man of Sino, to create bonds for what they believe to be projects, for humanity. All documents, receipts and any other paperwork administered between parties, is put in safekeeping. I found them to be good, honourable people. Eddy and I are still great friends today.

The Swissindo is not just a myth, as some may claim.

According to Swissindo, the Gold lives in Indonesia and the Credit comes from Switzerland.

It is also reported that the greatest hordes of Gold are under the Mountains in the Swiss Alps. Maybe, they both have the Gold and the Credit?

Are those claims true?

This goes much deeper than what it appears.

It is of great importance to learn about these 'systems' because they are all interlinked. Here are a few links to the 'systems';

The United Nations (UN)
The North Atlantic Treaty Organization (NATO)
The Bank for International Settlements (BIS)
The World Economic Forum (WE-Forum)

It is not just the organisations themselves but;

- Who owns them?
- Where does funding come from?
- Who are the sister, brother and cousin companies?
- What other 'businesses' do they align with?

Once you start looking and unearthing, wow!

During this second trip, I had the absolute honour of meeting up with three Royal families, who all owned large assets that were not held in the banks or the banking systems. Their assets are 'stashed' in various secret sites.

Royal Family of Thailand
- Meeting with Randall -

These Royal families were very impressed with my paperwork as they recognised my dear friend, Capilano. Capilano was a sovereign leader in Canada and this was the reason why they agreed to meet up with me in the first place. These families don't just meet with anybody, especially when it comes to discussing their treasure troves! They were highly fearful of their accumulated wealth and treasures. The Royals were of Muslim faith and during our conversations, they spoke their native language. I had my friend with me, who was translating and assisting me with our exchanges.

With one family, we invited them to put together an assay (measurement of gold), of their treasures to show the value and how much they had in total. We even suggested for them to quote a small portion of their wealth, if they had any fears or concerns. We assured them that we would give them a safekeeping receipt which is an 'esker'. This is bank terminology which gives one proof of where the assets reside and you can begin a credit line based on that. The banking system would allow and enable the owners of the esker to fund projects because they have something to back it with.

Does this make sense?

It's like saying, "Here's my paperwork for $1,000,000, please give me $100,000." The paperwork proves and identifies the asset you have. The bank then agrees to your request.

As I was enjoying my time at this gathering, one of the men stood up and left the room. He went outside to his vehicle and when he returned, he had brought me back a gift, it was a ring! He placed it on my finger and it actually fit! We hugged and took photos …but there was no marriage proposal!

It was big in size but not true Gold, although the gemstone had value.

Through the interpreter I cheekily asked "How much of this stuff have you got?" he replied with "My family alone has about 600 tonnes of wealth not very far from here." I was blown away!

Not by the accumulated wealth or treasures but by the whole situation. The whole scenario was surreal! It was ironic how Royalty had agreed to an informal and unofficial meeting with us, dressed, as I would describe it and just as a visual for you, as bums! They had missing or no teeth, their clothing was slightly unkempt in style but they were very clean and beautiful, all at the same time! I am not insulting them, I am stating a clear fact.

They are deeply religious people and their accumulated wealth affected them, in what I would call a 'sad way'. These people believed that if they touched, misused or spent any of their treasure, then Allah would strike them down. That's obviously why I got the ring made from metals and not real Gold. For me personally, it truly shows the power of their beliefs and from that realization, a simple question came up for me: "If these religious myths are passed onto the families, reminding them that their only job is to protect the treasures and the wealth, then who are they protecting it from?" It also feels like a heavy burden to me, with no pleasure or joy because of the deep fear attached to the Gold. Now, I understand their mind-set if the wealth is misused or abused, but not if it's used to benefit oneself and the 'greater good', this being the whole of humanity.

What are your thoughts on this?

Gold, silver, platinum, diamonds, oils and a long list of other treasures, simply exists on this remarkable planet called Earth. It has been here for aeons of time and also has been mined for good intentions and bad ones!

This underground treasure trove is in the roots of trees, in tunnels, miles of caves, amidst caverns, natural bunkers, under seas and oceans, under moist soils, buried in dry sands and any other area of this land. We have the honourable gift of being born into this wondrous planet and the beautiful gifts are for ALL beings, which exist here. Not just human beings but all beings. Animals, creatures, oceans, skies, feathered and winged friends, mountains, forests, insects, blossoms, etc.

Who gave permission to **mine** these precious items?

Isn't 'mine' an interesting word?

Whether you believe in God, Allah, Buddha, Krishna, Source, Creator, Infinite, Paganism, Atheism etc. ultimately, it ALL belongs to the Earth and if Earth owns its own creations, WHO has the right to put a value on these treasures?

So, what exactly is the **value** of these treasures?

Who made that 'value' story up?

Oh yes, I remember now···M.A.N. Men Among the Noble.

This isn't the real interpretation of the word 'MAN', I just made that one up!

Somewhere far down the line, things were decided for us without our AGreement. But what I do know and believe, is that during this century, we have become fully ingrained into a completely 'man-made system', that each of us were tricked into. We the people were misled, misused and misinformed.

Before I go further into my trip, I wish to share with you the beauty of this Indonesian island. The religion in Indonesia is mainly Muslim and the rest of the people are of Christian faith. These two religions appear to work well together and I can truly say that these people are some of the loveliest people I have met during my life. As you can see, I had so many opportunities to celebrate with these folk that surrounded me, whether I bumped into them in synchronised events or met with them at pre-arranged meetings. I was always honoured when I got invited to their mosques and participated in such beautiful ceremonies, where I felt so much love from their spiritual practices. The Indonesians are such wonderful people and I certainly would recommend you pop it on your wish-list, to visit sometime in the future.

During my stay, I settled in the same five-star hotel, which I used on both of my trips and can you believe that over the space of two years, the price stayed at $66 per night which included a breakfast buffet which was always exquisite, with a spread of stunning foods and delights.

My meetings were based in Pope Pius XII Catholic Center in Manila. This is where I conversed with government officials, municipal leaders and other people. Here, I was still promoting the Marcos accounts. I talked about this in the Victory Notes chapter. The names on the 'bonds' are the 'keepers' of those accounts and **not** the 'owners' of those accounts.

My next connection was with Raveeroj Rithchoteanan, who was from the Royal family of Thailand, a Thai monk who still, to this current day, is the CEO and President of the company 'Centennial Energy Thailand'. He was one of the holders of these accounts, as a legal entity. Raveeroj was attempting to bring funds into Angola, South Africa, from his accounts that were backed by the Central Bank of the Philippines'. This was where the Gold was backed by the Marcos accounts.

Raveeroj Tithchotean

When you chat to one person, then it leads onto another.

I also met up with the Cabinet Secretary of Infrastructure & Finance of the Philippines, Arthur Tugade, who is also the current Secretary of the Department of Transportation.

Arthur Tugade & the ladies with Randall

Cabinet Secretary of Agriculture

Most of the people I met along the way took me seriously because I could speak the banking language and it was obvious that I knew the information. There was meeting after meeting. But something deep inside of me knew that I had to make more of an effort, to get closer to Duterte.

Meeting with Direct Secretary at Malacanang Palace

Through another chain of events, I got to speak with one of Duterte's advisors who scheduled an appointment for me to meet a woman, who had the authority to schedule appointments with Duterte. Woo Hoo! Success!

I was able to get an appointment to meet with Duterte the very next day at 3pm. As you can imagine, the next morning I awoke with great excitement as I was finally going to meet the President himself!

But then something happened!

I suddenly got a message, that the Prime-minister of Canada, Justin Trudeau shook his finger at Duterte that exact day and said to him "Those helicopters we sold you are not going to be equipped with weapons."

Duterte wanted those helicopters to suppress Muslim uprisings that were initiated by the banking 'system'. He wanted to keep the Muslims from fighting the Christians. Those helicopters were designed to be sold for Duterte's plan to be put into action. But suddenly, everything changed in an instant when Justin Trudeau said that to him.

"Fuck you and your helicopters! Fuck every Canadian! I'm not meeting with that guy!" exclaimed Duterte.

My meeting was cancelled and I was like "Oh my god, this cannot be happening…I was so close!"

I remember this moment so vividly, as various events were all happening in unison, in a short space of time. I also received word that Raveeroj Rithchoteanan had been thrown into jail on the same day! It was February 24th 2018.

Why was Raveeroj thrown in jail?

I later discovered that Raveeroj was trying to work with government officials to fund his projects in Angola, while other government advisors wanted him and his associates, out of the way.

The bankers backing the standalone credit instruments Raveeroj was carrying, hesitated and this gave the ruling government a great opportunity to call 'foul' and start arresting people. Raveeroj was caught in a mess and the bankers threw him under the bus!

Three years later, he is still in Securities Exchange Commission (SEC) prison. His associates were freed just recently, in March of 2021. Raveeroj will soon be free. It was and has been nasty stuff.

During this morning madness, I then get a call from Bauer Rothschild (whom you will learn more about in Chapter 9 – Ownership of the People).

We were discussing all of the events that were happening and he simply said to me "You are so deep in this Bilderberg story and you're gonna get chucked in jail. Get the fuck home and stay out of it!" I replied back to him "I'm not fearful. If they were going to throw me in jail, they know where I am because you know where I am. I will take your advice and lay low." I did just that, I kept my nose clean as the saying goes. I met with a few other people and stayed another two weeks. I continued to study, research and learn more as I evaluated the current situations and my previous trip.

When we eventually returned home, Margaret and I tried numerous banks with our 50 million dollar bond but not **one** of them would AGree,

AUthenticate or AUthorise the standalone credit instrument that Henry had given to us, as a gift for humanity. I eventually threw the bond in the trash can, as we were getting nowhere and none of the banks would accept the bond. Maybe I was fed up with the whole thing at that exact moment but I have no regrets about the action I took.

For weeks after my trip, I was absorbing the details and compartmentalizing my experiences and I thought "How the fuck am I gonna tell the world this stuff? Nobody's gonna believe me!"

And this was what propelled me into creating my YouTube channel.

And my final addition to this chapter is some very interesting information that you can research further on. But here is a little taster!

Sukarno was the very first President of Indonesia, 1945-67. He was born Kusno Sosrodihardjo and many Indonesians still remember him as 'Bung Karno' or 'Pak Karno'. Sukarno was in collaboration and partnership with President John F. Kennedy. It is believed that they both knew the depth of the Swissindo and were making deals to bring the money back to the people by using the Gold as the collateral backing, as a new U.S. Treasury Note. This was prior to John F. Kennedy's assassination in 1968. It has been suggested that he was never actually killed but it was a fake assassination for him to go into hiding. In the future we will get to know the truth of what actually happened. On October 21st 2017, President Trump declared that he would unveil the classified files on the assassination of President John F. Kennedy, so we await the news!

"Then the shit hit the fan."
~ John Kenneth Galbraith - A Life in Our Times ~

7
Sulu Sea Collection

"Do not be alarmed by simplification, complexity is often a device for claiming sophistication, or for evading simple truths."
~ John Kenneth Galbraith ~

The Sulu Sea is a body of water in the southwestern area of the Philippines and this area of Mother Earth contains many islands. Actually, thousands of islands! Can you believe that? ⋯and in such a small area in the World too!

There are around 7,100 islands *around* the Philippines.

There are around 10,000 islands *around* Indonesia.

Some of these islands come right out of the water. Some of them don't even have a shore! With the addition of nature's elements, they can present perilous and dangerous travels on the seas. The ocean can be rough around these isles and islets. For thousands of years 'pirates' knew that the ships sailed here, carried their wealth aboard and the thieves were ready to steal it for themselves. Sometimes they even had ulterior motives, whether it was over a personal matter, a legacy or simply for their own greedy desires.

It is also believed that the land 'drowned' during the period of Lemuria and that world is now underground. This belief does hold some truth to it. Let me share some of my insights and history with you, not about Lemuria but more recently, from WWII.

Let's go back in time, to just *one* story from WWII… 'Yamashita's Gold'.

During the Second World War, Japan conquered vast sectors of the Pacific. They looted Gold, ancient artefacts and a variety of other riches. The Japanese army scavenged all of China and Southeast Asia including Thailand and Taiwan. By 1945, the Japanese knew that it was highly likely that they were going to lose the war, as the U.S. forces blocked the way to Japan. General Tomoyuki Yamashita, commander of the 14th Area Army, supposedly buried most or all of the treasure in the Philippines. It is believed that the treasure was hidden in 172 secret sites around the Philippines, in caves, tunnels and underground complexes, using prisoners of war as labour. Once everything was buried, General Yamashita surrendered. When the war ended, he was tried and quickly executed, taking his secret to the grave. The mystery of this 'lost' World War II treasure has not been solved for 70 years.

What do you think, dear reader?

Did someone get his access to his secret, before he died?

This is *one* of hundreds of thousands of many great mysteries of World Wars, even going back as far as the Lemurian times. No matter whether it's Gold, weapons, secrets, scrolls, artefacts, an endless list of treasures or even a combination of any of those that Yamashita hid underground, and whether you think it is a tale, myth or the complete truth in disguise. Just be assured that many politicians, leaders, elite families, popes and monarchs *know* of these hidden places. How about MI-5 and even the CIA?

Who were the past pirates?

Were they the sailors that wore patches over one eye who walked with wooden peg legs? Or were they the leaders of battalions and troops?

Who are the modern-day pirates?

Our governments? Our leaders? Royals wearing a crown?

Did you ever wonder what's under the earth, soil, mountains, sands and out to the seas? Not by inches or feet but by hundreds of metres and even miles below land level. There is such an expansive 'space' under our feet which is perfect for storage, safety and the security of valuable items where it is dry and has the perfect humidity and atmosphere below ground or under the seas. There is an abundance of territory to store treasures where others would never dream of looking, let alone have access to.

Let's stick to the simplicity of Gold.

It's the same old story where the 'elite' claim it and steal it for themselves and their family lineage and bloodline. They have done this for so long, we have lost track of them!

The Gold is *ours* to share amongst *all* of the people who reside on this Earth and it was never meant to be used for personal greed and corruption within government, monarchies, religious heads, corporate CEO's and 'privileged' organisations and companies.

Did you know that in 2020, around *62* plane loads of Gold were removed from the Vatican? Think about that for a moment.

Sixty two aeroplanes *full* of GOLD.

Am I 100% sure of this information?

No, I was not there in person but I'm confident it's a 99% possibility, with all of the information that I had access to!

It is believed that this was *one* of the main reasons for Italy being put into the 2020 global lockdown *first,* so that the Vatican could be extradited.

Earlier, in another chapter I mentioned that I did a video for my YouTube audience and I was questioning the numbers of cases. I was asking "Why are we in a lockdown for an estimated 0.05% death rate?"

This had nothing to do with an agreement or disagreement of the *lockdown*, I did this to share facts and data, for people to research. I just thought I would add this in, in case you were wondering…. Back to the Vatican!

Have you ever wondered about the Vatican in Vatican City?

Did you know that the Vatican City is officially a STATE?

It is independent from Italy, even though it's in the capital city of Rome.

The Pope in the Vatican is the head of the Catholic Church worldwide.

The Pope governs the Catholic Church through the 'Roman Curia'.

The Roman Curia comprises the administrative institutions of the 'Holy See'.

The 'Holy See' is the jurisdiction of the Bishop of Rome, this being the Pope.

The 'Holy See' maintains bilateral diplomatic relations with 183 'sovereign' states.

The 'Holy See' is *claimed* to be *not* the Vatican City but it certainly is all interlinked. The 'Holy See' maintains diplomatic relations with states. Foreign embassies are accredited to the 'Holy See' and it is the 'Holy See' that establishes treaties and concordats (which is interlinked with the Catholic Church i.e.: The Vatican!) with other sovereign entities. When necessary, the 'Holy See' will enter a treaty on behalf of Vatican City.

Let's kick the jargon aside. Simply put, they are one!

So, let's *take a deeper look at* who the 'Holy See' & the 'Vatican City' participates with, outside of prayers and incense!

They are members of various international organizations and groups. I have listed the larger ones but there are probably many more that you can find. This is a start:

The International Atomic Energy Agency (IAEA)
The International Organization for Migration (IOM)
The International Labour Organization (ILO)
The International Telecommunication Union (ITU)
The Organisation for the Prohibition of Chemical Weapons (OPCW)
The Organization for Security and Co-operation in Europe (OSCE)
The Organization of American States (OAS)

The United Nations (UN)
The United Nations High Commissioner for Refugees (UNHCR)
The United Nations General Assembly (UNGA)
The United Nations Educational, Scientific and Cultural Organization (UNESCO)
The United Nations Industrial Development Organization (UNIDO)
The United Nations Conference on Trade and Development (UNCTAD)
The United Nations Environment Programme (UNEP)
The United Nations Human Settlements Programme (UN-Habitat)

The World Trade Organization (WTO)
The Food and Agriculture Organization of the United Nations (FAO)
The African Union (AU) - wink wink!
The Arab League
The Council of Europe (CoE)

- The World Tourism Organization (UNWTO)
- The World Food Programme[a] (WFP)
- The World Health Organization (WHO)
- The World Intellectual Property Organization (WIPO)

Phew! Sounds like they're running the world!

Is this what they do for pleasure and leisure, aside from preaching?

Why would the Vatican City, which is just a religious faith in the Catholic Church, have such humongous connections and participation with these organisations, federations, agencies and councils?

I hope you take some time to research further and probe a little deeper, as I now return to the 62 plane loads of Gold.

Why do you think that Italy was put into a lockdown first?

I believe that this was done on purpose, so that the flights were obscured from public eyes and camouflaged for removal of the Gold from The Vatican City. It was done in disguise.

Do you know how shocking it would be for all of those thousands upon thousands of innocent people, in Rome alone to witness that?

Could you imagine the shock of any religious or non-religious person witnessing plane after plane, landing and departing on St. Peter's Square on the Basilica grounds. It may even create mass panic and mayhem because no mainstream media could account for it. That is, telling the people the truth.

Could you imagine a *newsflash* announcing that the Vatican and the whole of the Catholic Church never honoured God or Jesus Christ? But rather raped his name and truth, over and over for centuries! This FAITH crucified Jesus Christ, his beloved Mary Magdalene, their bloodline and the Essenes, which was a type of community of truth. The truth that God resides within us all and this is the place to find FAITH, BELIEF, TRUST & TRUTH. This Catholic Church lied about the Apostles and St. Peter, it was a complete deception from a Bible that has been edited and revised thousands of times.

This is a current day example:

In the Gospel of Matthew 16:19 – Jesus says to Peter,

> *"I will give you the keys of the kingdom of heaven, and whatever you bind on Earth shall be bound in heaven, and whatever you loose on Earth shall be loosed in heaven."*

Now I am not religious in the faith of a Church but I am in the faith of my soul, as a creator on this Earth. My perception of those words are that the keys are symbolic of the human soul being able to access something, like figuring out how to unlock a door if the key is not turning.

A key to a door.
Unlocking the mysteries.
Whatever is bound on Earth is bound in Heaven.
Whatever is lost on Earth is lost in Heaven.

Earth is Heaven and Earth can be Hell. There is no above and no below. There are no heavenly angels above and the demons below. It's all a metaphor to ALL. Everything is ONE. God is metaphysical not a human being. The mystical, esoteric and spiritual side of us, is a fundamental part of being human. The angels and demons *do* exist all around us every day but you have a choice, in essence, which one to believe in and follow in life. So, it makes sense to me that if you cannot find your love on Earth, then how can you find this anywhere else, if Earth is Heaven?

I know it's not as transparent or as straightforward as that but it helps to start back at the beginning and find an uncomplicated ground to work upon.
This Catholic Church is a *group*.
This Catholic Church is a *system*.
This Catholic Church is an *organisation.*
This Catholic Church assists the *'elite'.*

This 'church' has betrayed us with Science, the Universe, Planetary Systems, Sacred World Sites and on and on and on.

I am so grateful to be alive to watch these 'systems' dissolve before my eyes and you too will see, over the coming decades, how our kind and loving hearts will evolve into the 'Heaven on Earth' that God intended and not the 'Hell on Earth' *they* created. This old 'system' is now becoming our *History*!

Jesus Christ did come from a *bloodline* and if you take some time on this, you can look into its history and your eyes will be opened wide.

Why?

Because you will see the way marriages were originally arranged, in essence, to contribute to material gain and capitalisation in the genes for offspring and thus continuation of politics, leadership, religion or monarchies.

Jesus Christ did not *marry* in the church, Jesus and Mary Magdalene merged themselves with blessings, celebrations and an undeniable unity, which only exists in the heart and expands from that space. This is called LOVE.

Jesus Christ & Mary Magdalene

"Let it be emphasized once more, and especially to anyone inclined to a personally rewarding scepticism in these matters: For practical purposes, the financial memory should be assumed to last, at a maximum, no more than 20 years. This is normally the time it takes for the recollection of one disaster to be erased and for some variant on previous dementia to come forward to capture the financial mind. It is also the time generally required for a new generation to enter the scene, impressed, as had been its predecessors, with its own innovative genius."

~ John Kenneth Galbraith - A Short History of Financial Euphoria ~

8
The 'Elite' Bloodline

"If you feed enough oats to the horse, some will pass through to feed the sparrows" (Referring to "trickle down" economics).
~ John Kenneth Galbraith ~

There are assorted titles given by our current society to segregate the 'elite' families, here are some of those titles that may be recognisable to you but not necessarily words that I would use.

The Cabal
Illuminati
Deep State
New World Order
Black Hats

Some say that there are 13 bloodlines which have connections to wealth and power that are simply unimaginable. These families are World Wide! They are not just families but 'Houses' that go back far in time.

"Some even believe we are part of a secret cabal working against the best interests of the United States, characterizing my family and me as 'internationalists' and of conspiring with others around the world to build a more integrated global political and economic structure – one world, if you will. If that's the charge, I stand guilty and I am proud of it."

~ David Rockefeller ~

In 1882, John D Rockefeller set up one of the first investment management businesses, designed to run a single family's income. Simply creating a business of slavery through the everyday family.

It's a structure in an infrastructure.

The 'elite' hold the Magistrates and courthouses, governments and the constabulary, the whole educational institution, natural resources, foreign policies, food production, national economies, media houses, even terrorist organisations and more!

So, who apparently are these 13 bloodlines? Is the 13 a myth or factual?

I will share with you first, my research and then follow on with my truth.

The most powerful *house* is Marquis de Libeaux then followed by:

I. Rothschild's-Bauer (Ashkenazi Jews)
II. Bruce (Scotland)
III. Cavendish (Anglo-Normans)
IV. de Medici (Italian)
V. Hanover (German)

VI. Hapsburg (Austria)
VII. Krupps (German)
VIII. Plantagenet (France)
IX. Rockefeller (American)
X. Romanov (Russia)
XI. Sinclair/St. Clair (Scotland)
XII. Warburg-del Banco (Venetian Jewish to German Jewish)
XIII. House of Windsor (United Kingdom)
   ➢ Triad/Dragon (China) - some may call these the 'stooges' that work alongside these bloodlines.

Here are some additional bloodlines linked to those families, let's see if you recognise any of them.

i. Astor
ii. Bundy
iii. Collins
iv. DuPont
v. Freeman
vi. Kennedy
vii. Li
viii. Onassis
ix. Reynolds
x. Russell
xi. Van Duyn

*"I care not what puppet is placed on the throne of England to rule the Empire.
The man who controls Britain's money supply controls the British Empire
And I control the British money supply."*

~ Nathan Mayer Rothschild ~

These top thirteen families stand eligible in terms of their financial, political, and historical background as they are associated with and belong to various secret societies and cult groups like the Council of Thirteen, Freemasons, The Skull and Bones, The Rosicrucians, The Elders of Zion, and Bilderberg.

Bilderberg is a very tiny organisation which manipulates and exploits the governments worldwide; now you know where the expression comes from "our hands are tied."

These families 'pull the strings' of the 'puppets' beneath them, but are not the ones who actually threaten the governments, royals and leaders in military or other positions. They don't even put them in compromising situations! Rather it's the 'system' these families have created, that oversees these governments, etc. These controlling families know that the people inside these 'systems' will manage each other and basically, fuck each other over. At the higher levels there is corruption and exploitation with either collusion or sexual blackmail, using manipulation of the human being by means of hookers, paedophilia, drugs, fraud, etc.

"Oh yes, you will follow our rules" they say and it really is that simple in the course of these structures of creation. *'They'* made it that way so that once you were in, there was no way out! The planners and the schemers are the 'minions' or the 'stooges' and then the ladder of authority lessens but the 'game' still gets played, working its way down the ladder to the general public.

Come on…how many movies have you seen where the right hand man gets shot in the skull! And then everyone is watching their backs and not trusting anyone and eventually they all get hammered, one after another.

There are a few people that are 'in the know' of this *system*, who don't get sucked in or paid off. I will give you an example shared by a former politician, Doctor Dave Janda, who was being interviewed on the SGT Report. He shares a story of when he was told by a fellow politician to always avoid going to private parties. The advice was telling Janda, if he was ever invited to a private party by anyone in the political circles, including events at the Vice President's residence, to *always* decline the request!

He was advised only to go to a party if it's at the White House and of course, if you're invited by the President.

The 'private parties' were 'set ups' so *they* could drug these politicians and whilst the individual was in a drugged state, they would have pictures taken of that political figure having sex with an underage kid and other types of scenarios. Once these doped up politicians awoke from their intoxicated stupor, they'd find a polaroid picture on their chest showing the footage, that they were now going to be blackmailed with. It was easy to blackmail these politicians from that point onwards. Dr. Janda went on to say that he found out, in speaking with the fellow politician who gave him the advice not to go to these parties, that there were over 90% of politicians being 'set up' like this or in some other blackmail traps.

This was back in the late 1980's! Janda went on to say that today that number is now probably over the 99% plateau.

Do you think this is shocking?

Or is it expected?

So, now it's my turn to share with you, my personal list from the men in the know!

These are the TTb's - Top Twelve banks.

The TTb project or some call it, the Top Thirty-six banks, represent 330,000 banks internationally (3% of businesses).

This list I share with you has been given to me by my banking friends. The line-up is the 12 Family bloodlines and the banks that they own and who you may even bank with!

- Bauer-Rothschild - Barclays
- Brown- Harriman - NatWest (RBS - Royal Bank of Scotland)
- Rothschild and Lord - Citigroup (London domiciled)
- Warburg - SBC Warburg Bank of Hamburg (includes Warburg Bank of Amsterdam)
- Lazard Brothers - Banque Fédérative du Crédit Mutuel (Paris)

- Israel Moses Seif - Unicredit (Banks of Italy)
- Goldman Sachs - Goldman Sachs ([London domiciled])
- Lehman Brothers - Lehman Bros ([London domiciled])
- Kuhn Loeb - Kuhn Loeb Bank ([London domiciled])
- Bundy - BNP Paribas
- Bilderberg (Bilderberger) - Credit Suisse (Switzerland) control US Presidency since Lyndon Baines Johnson
- Rockefeller - HSBC (London domiciled)

If I have not mentioned a bank that you use, then it will be a company somewhere along the line and linked to one of them.

Remember that these are Non-Orthodox 'cousin' banks to the Orthodox Banks. You can see who you do retail business and if you do your research on the 'Top 100 International Banks', you will find Chinese Banks leading the way, with their population-based credit schemes.

You have to realise that YOU are the creditors and WE as a collective, have to re-create the current system otherwise we will keep cycling around with no exit point. The *worst* thing that we can do, in my opinion, is to BLAME these governments and officials because it's not going to help us create the significant change that is needed. I don't agree with the idea of 'hanging' or 'tribunals' for a death sentence, unless it's a kind of apprehension. I don't think anyone deserves to have their head cut off either but I know this happens.

A tactic that can be used is to give the person a timescale to expose 'full disclosure' of any of their associates, partners, etc, rather than convict that person to an immediate death. This gives the interrogators the opportunity to shed light on the corruption and evil that the individual was linked to. I am sure there is an assortment of methods to coerce, blackmail, torment, spook and intimidate someone to confess, declare, divulge and reveal the necessary details required. This makes more sense to me, to take the time and get what you want from the internal store of truth because if that person is dead, then they will take it with them to their graves and then you are going to be limited in unveiling the full deception and the line of people attached to that one person.

I choose to go no further on this subject in this chapter, as there is a plethora of open information to view on the web. And it's also based on your beliefs on how people need to be 'sentenced' and I am not here to debate these stories, just to share my knowledge and wisdom with you. Go where you choose to tread.

For myself, those 'elite' have GONE and the minions are now scrambling to find sanctuary and are full of fear. They are trying to stay alive in the best way that they can. The whole structure is collapsing and has now finally…FAILED!

It is time for arrests and revelations, step-by-step. But I still feel that you must treat an enemy with compassion and wisdom. If you dive in and scream, they will go into panic and fear and go with desperate measures to keep afloat for the truth NOT to be REVEALED. There is no need to go in with the pitchforks and flaming torches chanting for them to 'pay-the-price' and 'hang for their sins'.

This opens up opportunities for the true leaders to lead. Leaders who are conscious of humanity, loving and come in peace.

These LEADERS are the everyday people in all stages of life.

This means YOU.
This means ME.
The Humanitarians.
The Truth Seekers
The Truth Givers.

The compassionate souls.

The ones who know there is more to live for.

YOU have the projects.
YOU have the visions.
YOU have the ideas.
YOU have the LOVE.

We need YOU.

ALL OVER THE WORLD

DON'T STOP

DO NOT DAMPEN YOUR SPARK

DO NOT DIM YOUR LIGHT

DO NOT DARKEN YOUR MAGNIFICENCE

YOU HAVE POWER TO CREATE FREEDOM

I hope you have gained insight from my experiences that I have shared with you to this point. After knowing this truth and information for such a long time, it was like "I gotta tell the people!"

I'm going to take a few more steps back to a time where I gained some assets and then lost those same assets.

I had been a cattle rancher for three decades and was now in the process of losing my business and my home. The 'Courts of Law' took me on a trail that astounded me. I never knew what Common Law meant until I represented myself without the help of any lawyers, over a period of three years. We are disillusioned if we believe that the people and the public are to follow Marshall Law···this was another trip down the yellow brick road to meet the Wizard of Oz!

Are you gonna join me?

Great!

In the next chapter, before I get into sharing the *whole* story of going to the courthouse, you need to know a little more about the various Laws, Bonds & Trusts and how your personal Tax Identification and Birth Certificates are all interlinked.

*"There are two kinds of forecasters:
Those who don't know, and those who don't know they don't know."*

~ John Kenneth Galbraith ~

116

9
Ownership of the People

"The process by which money is created is so simple that the mind is repelled. Where something so important is involved, a deeper mystery seems only decent."
~ John Kenneth Galbraith ~

Let me keep it simple, Marshall Law –v- Maritime Law –v- Common Law.

L = Land

A = Air

W = Water

Marshall Law:

Martial law is an extreme and rare measure used to control society during war or periods of civil unrest or chaos.

Maritime Law:

The body of legal rules that governs ships and shipping.

Common Law:

The body of law created by judges and similar quasi-judicial tribunals by virtue of being stated in written opinions.

Or, in simple terminology:

'The common sense of the community, crystallised and formulated by our forefathers'.

Now then.

Why oh why, are we led to believe the LAW - in all areas of the world from the Courts of Law, Assets, Marriage, Death and all various Certificates BUT to abide only by Maritime Law?

This is vital information that *every* human needs to know.

Why?

This is *your* FREEDOM as a human being, residing on this great plane-t.

It continues throughout *your* life! It begins from *your* BIRTH until the time of *your* DEATH and even beyond that, if it involves property, wealth, paperwork, etc.

The banking families, the 'elite', the cabal, or whatever phrase feels right for you to use, created the 'legal jurisdiction' *laws*. All of the laws to suit the 'groups' that *they* too also created, such as Kings & Queens, Prince & Princesses, Dukes & Duchesses, Lords & Ladies, Barons & Baronesses, etc. THEY have been around for centuries and beyond! The history of that structure alone is very deep and mind-blowing. However, rather than going into that, I will remain on the subject matter of ownership and keeping to the most recent of times, where we focus mainly on Europe and paying *particular* attention to the 'British Crown'.

So, my next question to you is, "What assets do believe you own?"

A few decades ago, I lived in a world of Capitalism, speculating on land, buying and selling cattle. I wanted to create a bigger business and enhance the value chain, taking the beef from my cattle, right through to retail and I knew that I had the potential to do this on a large scale. Back then, I was still thinking in terms of investments and investors. My mind had no understanding of unlimited resources, when it came to credit and money.

So, when I lost my assets by taking some *chances* in that financial world and thus failing to get the investments that I needed, I asked a very important question to my bank "Where is my original wet ink signed document?" The bank couldn't give those documents back to me but I *knew* they <u>couldn't</u> give them back to me. I also knew that those papers carried value, which was the promise from *my* AUtograph which allowed the bank to create the credit through me.

So, why did I ask for this document in the first place?

Well, it came into my awareness from various conversations with different people concerning the 'Birth Certificate Bond' meaning that YOUR Birth Certificate is an actual Bond. In the current system, we, as individuals, are <u>not</u> the holders of our own Birth Certificates. We are only allowed to get 'certified copies' of our certificate. That way, we can never be the actual holder of the bond.

After the certification of our *live birth* is applied for and issued, no one ever sees it again. Thus, our certificate of live birth is taken from us and negotiable *instruments* are issued from it. And these instruments are traded on the stock market. Your Birth Certificate has a serial number on it and it is the equivalent, in fiat currency, of our birth weight in Gold that is put into a *trust*.

So, YOUR Birth Certificate is a 'Bond'!

Is this clear enough for you?
YOUR Birth Certificate is a 'Bond'!

All of the information that I share with you, is not to provoke rebellion, hostility, disorder or turmoil for you to reclaim your rightly-owned wealth but to enlighten you, as a living human being, to the reality of this world in which you live in, both in its reverence of the light and in the shadows of the dark.

Some people call this Bond - the STRAWMAN.

When a parent/s or guardian registers the birth of a child, this procedure declares the child *falsely* as 'dead' or/and 'lost at sea'. This is why it is called a birth = *berth*. You have now become cargo and you have been *delivered out* to sea. The AUtograph from the adult agrees to send you out to sea! How crazy is that?! Few people are aware of this because it is *hidden* and if the 'elite' disclosed the truth to you, as you rocked up to get your child certified, I am sure you would walk away laughing, with a "No, thanks!"

Unbeknownst to the individual registering the State Birth Certificate, this sets up a *hidden* TRUST as a *fictional* account with the Government, being the *trustee*. This is where Maritime Law is forced onto the people as in a LAW that we must obey but it's *fake* because in truth, you are a *dead* person at sea and not a *living* human being on land!

I will let you absorb all of this for a moment, maybe go back and re-read what I have just stated.

My dear friend, Anna Von Reitz, explains this beautifully and I certainly advocate her content of knowledge on this subject.

Let's jump to your adult identification number that exists in all countries for governmental tax purposes and is there to keep everything in order....or is it?

When a child reaches the numerical age of fifteen, the individual, in my home country of Canada, is issued a Social Insurance Number (SIN). In America an Internal Revenue Service (IRS), a social security number is issued and in Great Britain, this is named as a National Insurance number (NI). I know that there are tax systems in *all* countries but these are specifically connected with the US & UK Treasury. These numbers, once given to 'slaves' of the applicable country, it's a ticket or pass that grants you access to all the programs and services currently offered, by that particular government. This also means that the slave = you, is subject to all applicable fees and taxes for services, provided by being a holder of such a number...that's why on all the government statements and cards, your name is in all caps as you are a dead figure to them. The IRS is more like the bill-collector for the government...except in the US the IRS money does not go to America but rather to Great Britain!

With *your* personalised unique sorting code and *your* Birth Certificate, it becomes an access point to your Babylon Trust via the Vatican.

What is the Babylon Trust?

It's a charity based in England and connected to Her Majesty Queen Elizabeth II. It is a Charity with the number: 1136944 - which is a channel to the Babylon Trust Limited, with the company number: 07046224. This is linked to the Companies House, which is the UK's registrar of companies and is an executive *agency* and *trading funds* of Her Majesty's Government.

This is a TRUST.

How is this linked to the Vatican?

Unam Sanctam.

Unam Sanctam is a Papal Bull.

A Papal Bull is a Public Decree.

This Public Decree can only be issued by a Pope of the Catholic Church, hence the Vatican.

The first (apparent) Papal Bull was declared in 1302 by Pope Boniface VIII. Which laid down a church doctrine proposal for uniting the Catholic Church, as they believed that this was necessary for our eternal salvation. He was the first 'leader' to create the concept of a TRUST, which is a BOND.

The first Testamentary Trust, through a Deed and Will creating a Deceased Estate, was created by Pope Nicholas V in 1455, through the Papal Bull - Romanus Pontifex.

This Papal Bull had the effect of conveying the right of use of the land as Real Property, from the Express Trust - 'Unam Sanctam', to the *control* of the Pontiff and *his* successors in perpetuity.

Hence, ALL land is claimed as 'Crown Land'.

So, this '1st Crown' is represented by the 1st Cestui Que Vie Trust Act 1666, created when a child is born. It deprives us of all beneficial entitlements and rights on the land.

I know! It gets even better, keep reading!

Now, the '2nd Crown' is of the CommonWealth

The second crown or deeds of the second Testamentary Trusts, which was created by Pope Sixtus IV in 1481 with the Papal Bull - 'Aeterni Regis', meaning "Eternal King/Crown".

This Papal Bull created the "Crown of Aragon", later known as the Crown of Spain, and is the highest sovereign and highest steward of all Roman Slaves, subject to the rule of the Roman Pontiff. Spain lost the crown in 1604 when it was granted to King James I of England by Pope Paul V after the successful passage of the "Union of Crowns", or Commonwealth in 1605, after the false flag operation of the Gunpowder Plot. This Treason Plot or the Jesuit Treason, was a failed assassination attempt against King James I, by a group of provincial English Catholics led by Robert Catesby who sought to restore the Catholic monarchy from the Church of England after decades of Anglican ruling. The scheme was to blow-up the English parliament on the 5th of November 1605 to kill King James and as many members of Parliament as possible. This is 'Guy Fawkes' night. It is a night to celebrate with the family and a community, where we build a fire and set fire to the *straw-man* on top, who committed treason.

Have you ever wondered why we do what we do, in these rituals passed down?

Why would we set fire to an artificial man for fun?!

Why do we get the fireworks and sparklers out, to celebrate his death?

Because ultimately what is the truth?

Did Robert Catesby commit treason?

Who was doing the treachery, King James?

The politicians?

Maybe Robert and his allies knew the TRUTH and all these years, Guy Fawkes was being remembered for all of the wrong reasons…he sounds like a Hero to me!

What do you think?

It's similar to the Catherine Wheel, which was also known as the Breaking Wheel. In history, this was a used as a medieval torturing device, for public capital punishment. Maybe they thought Catherine was a 'witch' or maybe Catherine was a very wise woman and knew the TRUTH of the 'elite'. I love questioning the narrative, it certainly expands the mind. Now, back to the second crown.

Robert Catesby – Guy Fawkes

The Crown was finally lost by England in 1975, with my research, when it was returned to Spain and in the hands of King Carlos I, where it remains to this day. This 2nd Crown is represented by the 2nd Cestui Que Vie Trust. Created when a child is born and, by the sale of the birth (berth) certificate as a *Bond* to the private central bank of the nation. Depriving *us* of ownership of *our* own flesh and condemning *us,* to perpetual servitude, as a Roman person, or slave.

The Vatican is connected to the CommonWealth of England.

Read on…

The '3rd Crown'.

The third Crown was created in 1537 by Pope Paul III, through the Papal Bull 'Convocation', also meant to open the Council of Trent. It is the third and final testamentary Deed and Will of a Testamentary Trust, set up for the claiming of all "lost souls", lost to the sea. The Venetians assisted in the creation of the 1st Cestui Que Vie Act of 1540, to use this papal bull as the basis of Ecclesiastical authority of Henry VIII. This Crown was secretly granted to England in the collection and "reaping" of lost souls. The Crown was lost in 1816, due to the deliberate bankruptcy of England, and granted to the Temple Bar which became known as the Crown Bar, or simply the Crown. The Bar Associations have since been responsible for administering the "reaping" of the souls of the lost and damned, including the registration and collection of Baptismal certificates representing the souls collected by the Vatican and stored in its vaults.

This 3rd Crown is represented by the 3rd Cestui Que Vie Trust, created when a child is baptized. It is the parents' grant of the Baptismal certificate--title to the soul--to the church or Registrar. Thus, without legal title over one's own soul, we will be denied legal standing and will be treated as things--cargo without souls--upon which the BAR is now legally able to enforce Maritime law.

That was a lot of history for you to digest but I felt it was important to see *clearly* the links to the Vatican, Crowns, Governments, Political and Banking Systems. Simply put, it's all ONE.

Enjoy your future times, delving deeper into this magnificently hidden treasure of truths. It's hidden no more and it's in plain sight for anyone to find and see.

Back to those digits and ID's - which do remind me of the tattoos stamped on our true heroes in WWII, which I will touch upon in another chapter.

Those numbers and letters you have been given will verify with HMRC that, your personal unique banking codes are linked *to* and traded *from* HMRC. This stands for *He*r *M*ajesty's *R*evenue & *C*ustoms which is a non-ministerial department of the United Kingdom's Government that is responsible for the collection of taxes and the payment of some forms of state support. It is also the administration of other regulatory regimes which includes the national minimum wage and the issuance of National Insurance numbers.

HMRC issues your Birth Certificate Number and can be seen as a BOND on the Treasury Direct System.

HMRC and HM (Her Majesty's) Treasury are listed *companies* allowing *your* accounts to be traded because they are Trustees to *your* accounts. This also relates to the American bank, Citibank.

So, why would a UK corporation use an American bank?

Citibank is the consumer division of financial services of the multinational Citigroup. Citibank was founded in 1812 as the City Bank of New York, and later became First National City Bank of New York. The bank has 2,649 branches in 19 countries and is owned by the US Bloomberg Group. So, have you ever asked the question "Who owns my Bank?" "Who owns the Federal Reserve?" "Are they connected?" "Is the UK connected to the USA?"

So many questions!

It roughly started at the beginning of the 20th century where it appeared that America was in full swing with business and industries. However, unbeknownst to the hard-working citizens, the Government was in trouble. Bankruptcy was on the cards and this was not the first time either.

In 1907, a severe financial panic jolted Wall Street and forced several banks into failure. This panic, however, did not trigger a broad financial collapse. Yet the simultaneous occurrence of general prosperity with a crisis in the nation's financial centres, persuaded many Americans that their banking structure was sadly out-of-date and in need of major reform. So, basically several elite men attended a secret meeting in order to draw up a plan to *trick* the American people, which allowed a central bank into the country. Because of this meeting, the Federal Reserve was born.

They are buying and selling the shares in YOUR trust to make money for *their* clients. I am not telling you anything but I am sharing with you that this is 100% factual and if you feel like researching, then go ahead! It is getting easier and easier to access this data online, as so many people are seeing the truth by using the numbers and letters from their Birth Certificates and National Insurance Numbers and popping them into links that are accessible.

I know someone who is 51 years of age and when they put the data in from their Birth Certificate, they found that they had been traded on 758,000 times! Yes, you read that correctly, seven hundred and fifty eight thousand times on the stock market and the last recent trade was by Marks & Spencer, in 2021. She did have a moment when she felt like going into the store and saying to them, as she filled her trolley, "Everything that I put in this trolley is already paid for, as you owe me an estimated £500,000 and this store could not be here without me because of how you trade off me!" Thankfully, it was a moment of rage that passed. Rage can be a natural reaction as would feelings of disgust, shock, disturbance and distaste at the discovery of such a truth. It's not irrational but acceptable. But ultimately, it is wiser to embrace your emotions and thoughts and let them pass in their own time and their own way, without resorting to violence or any kind of attack to the corporations and organisations. Justice will prevail.

LIVE BIRTH RECORD TITLE CREATED BY "LIFE" >	BIRTH CERTIFICATE TITLE CREATED BY STATE
Baby Born, Endowed	Cargo Berthed, Delivered
Your **Mother** autographs to establish that you are "holder of your Estate in due course"	**Informant** autographs as indictment that you have no paternal holder of your Estate
Mother gives maiden name which indicates a bastard, later "still-born" on the Register	Registrar signs your Estate into Probate and you become a "Ward of the State"
Given a Lawful Name A lawful Given Name is **privately recorded**, traditionally in a Family name Bible	**Name is Corporatised** A legal Tradename is **publicly registered**, combining your Given and Family names
TITLE (Your Given Name)	CORPORATION (Tradename)
Rightful **Beneficiary** of the tradename	Unwitting **Trustee** of the tradename
Format is hand-written in proper grammatical English. Later usage shows your title as unique – John: (of family name)	Format is either hand-written or typed, and not necessarily all-capitals, which is often later used to indicate the legal name
'Capitis diminutio minima. The lowest or least comprehensive degree of loss of status. Rights of **liberty** and citizenship unaltered.' [Black's Law, 2nd Edition]	'Capitis diminutio maxima. The highest or most comprehensive loss of status. Changed from one of freedom to one of **bondage**.' [Black's Law, 2nd Edition]
SOVEREIGN PUBLIC TRUST At the age of 18 you can become Executor of your Estate as a free man/woman in your Sovereign Trust. As the "holder in due course", in a Permanent Trust, you can now at any time claim "Legal Title" to your Estate property	**FOREIGN SITUS TRUST** A Trust is formed by splitting your Estate, creating a "Legal Title" (holder) for the State, and an "Equity Title" (user) for you. As it is a Temporary not permanent Trust, you only have "possession" "use" not "Legal Title" of property
You are BENEFICIARY of SOVEREIGN PUBLIC TRUST State is your **Public Servant/Trustee** with a Fiduciary duty to protect and serve you, the rightful Beneficiary of your **Public Trust**	**State is BENEFICIARY of FOREIGN SITUS TRUST** State is **Holder** of your Estate (all property), used as a Surety for IMF debt obligations, and is the Beneficiary of the **Situs Trust**
Born as Holder of Estate, Creditor	Berthed as User of Estate, Debtor
This **Record** is used as Evidence for a Birth Certificate that certifies a Bond issue	This **Certificate** is certification of a Bond with the World Bank as Settlor of the Trust
Includes your birth weight in ounces used to calculate value in tables related to gold	The settled Bond becomes a Security that is traded on the Market for your value
Inhabitant Born on land with Inherent Jurisdiction and under Common **Law of the Land**	**Foreigner** Alien under Commercial Jurisdiction and later also Admiralty Maritime **Law of the Sea**
This document established your Estate, which can then be stolen. But it is also your Affidavit of Life and proof of claim	This document converts your Estate into a tradeable property and puts you to work for the Foreign Situs Trust via the "NAME"
Inherent Right to TITLE You are Holder of your Soveriegn Estate	**TITLE Claimed by State** False presumptions, claim and contract

So, let me get back to my original story and why I wanted my original wet ink papers back from the Bank. The term 'wet signature' refers to someone placing a physical signature or distinct mark on a hard copy of a document, with a pen or seal to make it legally binding.

As I was finding out more and more, I also came across the Common Law 'Pure' Trust (CLT) and Common Law Jurisdiction. The CLT is generally referred to simply, as a trust. It's a financial agreement by which a person or other entity (the trustee or settlor) transfers ownership of assets to another person or entity (the trustee) through the creation of a trust deed. The trustee is responsible to distribute benefits derived from the assets held in the trust (the trust fund), to at least one trust beneficiary when certain conditions are met.

Simply put, Common Law "Pure" Trust which is a 400-year-old document removes the trustee and places the 'trust' in the hands of the Managing Director, who is the original owner of the assets. It's a complex manner of remaining in control without owning any asset.

So, who is connected to the Common Law "Pure" Trust and that 400-year-old document?

Dr. Lord Grantham Taylor, Hughes, J.d., L.c.m.D, PH.D, Baron Von Bauer - Rothschild. Ongoing I shall name him as *Bauer*.

This man is a lawyer, broker and banker. Bauer also revises this 400-year-old document on behalf of the banking families. He also rewrites Wikipedia which is a Foundation. In addition to his talents, he also has access and edits our Dictionaries! Bauer has an IQ of 270. Now, that is what I call a Brainiac! Revising and reviewing history to suit current times, which I do believe could be altering, registering, recording and narrating a limited or optional truth to the chronicles of the past!

This *one* man acts upon changing data and we comply.

How do I know this?

He was another 'teacher' in my life.

I came across him when Margaret had made contact with him via email. She had found his information on the web and got no response. I was curious about this guy and so I emailed him myself and pursued with a few more messages. Eventually he replied to me and we conversed for a time, with emails going back and forth. Then one day, his response was "Call me" and added his telephone details for contact. Of course, I took the opportunity and dialled the number. Bauer took me seriously when I asked questions about the trusts and other information. I was intrigued and he even asked me if I wanted to get into the *'business'* with him and I replied "By all means, let's do it!"

And over many months, I absorbed lots of data about 'sovereign money creation' and its theories of a person's AUtographs and AGreements and the fact that an MT103 – a standalone credit instrument, is how credit is created – bank to bank – without anything but the Agreement, between the two banks and there is *NO-THING* to back it but the energy of the Banker, who AUtographs and AGrees with the wording. When he first said that to me, I was taken aback and I asked him "So, your family's money. Is that what backs it?" Bauer's family runs and manages

Barclays Bank (which is one of the top 100 banks) in two different banking structures, which are the 'ON-ledger accounts' and the 'OFF-ledger accounts'.

One that HOLDS the assets AWAY from the economy.
One that FLUCTUATES the assets IN the economy.

All the intelligence I ever needed was in his brain and he was feeding it to me!

> Me: "So then, this message of the MT103 *swift* message, has nothing to back it but the AGreement and the AUtograph of the people?"
> Bauer: "Human energy."

This makes so much sense to me. I love to break down the letters of words that we use as language because it can have hidden meanings, similar to a code or codex. So the word money, I believe, is the energy of the human being.

M
O
N
E
Y
=
My
Own
Net
Energy
Yield

Say it out loud a few times, it creates a new language!

I am not twisting the meaning around to disillusion you but showing you what is behind letters, words and its optional or true meaning. Words which originally came from the 'elite'.

Have you ever noticed or observed the way we use words?

What do they actually mean?

We seem to use speech but never question the words we express in our everyday language. We were just taught by our elders, parents, schools and the various 'systems' that were put in place and we just put our complete trust in the whole thing!

My time was coming to an end with Bauer. He had told me of his own personal frustrations with his family and projects that he wished to pursue, that were unsupported by his relations. He had previously broken away from his family, for a term of seven years. He went to India and spent time developing his spirituality because he was overdoing the demands from his family. He wanted to step away from the intellectual side of him and enter into another experience. He returned in good health and stepped back into his previous role, with a completely different outlook but combining his past knowledge. I am not saying he was illuminated to become the good out of the bad, I just know he was experimenting with new ideas and visions. I believe he is a GateKeeper, from a line bred genetic mutation of bloodlines. With his new experiments, he offered me $50 million dollars to join his venture but I declined this offer, as my unpaid commission for a brokerage deal that I had put together for his bankers left us at odds, and with that, he never made contact with me again.

You have all heard of the game Monopoly, I assume.

All I am doing is showing you how to play the *proper* game and not the original board game. I have also given you an upgrade for the instruction booklet, so that each person wins! Whether there are two players or six players, you will all receive a good outcome BUT only if you read the newly revised manual first!

I know that some of you reading these words may feel like 'WTF' or 'FFS'. Maybe you feel another negative sense of stupidity or shame for not recognizing the betrayal. Maybe you feel like a complete joke, falling for something so ridiculous! DON'T - You are a beautiful human being with a heart of love, compassion and forgiveness. You're sweet and honest and all you did was put your TRUST in the 'systems' because it was all you knew and all that your ancestors knew. This is why the 'elite' does this to a human soul because they do not recognize what LOVE is. They are the opposite, there is no-love. They are empty inside and feed off what they cannot ever have and that is YOU dear one.

YOU are the LOVE.

The beauty of the human soul was being tricked for trade.

I will keep reassuring and reiterating to you dear, that this is now not their world anymore and it cannot change overnight but the change has been administered for years and it's getting stronger and faster for each individual, to know their HUMAN RIGHTS on EARTH.

I am the Change.

You are the Change.

We are the Change.

Great team work ahead!

I also use the periodic table to open and expand your mind further.

AU = Gold

AG = Silver

PB = Lead

SB = Antimony

AU = Gold = Credit - 'AUthor'-isation - AUthentic - 'AUto'-graph

AG = Silver = *AGree*-ment

PB = Primary Banking = Lead = *Lead* to the Gold

SB = Secondary Banking = Antimony = *Anti-Money* = Creates the idea of 'debt'

Let me break it down even more for you.

This *credit instrument* is a stand of its own = a standalone credit instrument, which is the Author-isation of credit.

- Credit = Author-isation * recognition * approval.
- Instrument = legal * official * written.
- Credit instrument = bank note * cheque * bond * letter.
- Credit instrument = guarantees payment of a specific amount to a specific person.

§ PB = Primary Banking, which creates 'credit' from the AGreement.

So, unbeknownst to you, you are signing over to them, your silver and Gold!

§ SB = Secondary Banking, which creates the *idea* of 'debt'.

So unbeknownst to you, you are inviting debt and declining money!

So, there is no 'debt' just the idea of it···wow! It blew my mind!

Is your intellect accepting this information?

We are currently going through a huge transition which is leading us into a 'new' system, that will take some time for adjustment and to be in the collective and in our mainstream lifestyles. It's an 'old' idea that requires patience and step-by-step experience and understanding. We have to restructure the belief system of money of our Birth Certificate Bonds, Common Law Trusts, Common Law Jurisdiction and more. But the most important part is that we the people, are not allowing the 'elite' families to run the world anymore. There are unlimited resources and funding coming from *off-ledger* accounts and these are HUGE accounts that can change the economy of the world! The Central Banks 'funnelled' the money, meaning they limited it for the people. The 'funnel' effect will become a 'pipe' effect, for the people. Straight through.

This is not a conspiracy and it's not theory nor are the 'elite' the bad guys here necessarily, it was just the way the 'system' was set up.

Is that completely wrong?

I would say "no" as there is a certain amount of organisation within the system and its process. As a 'Public Organisation', or another term generally used is the 'Government', the duty is to the people as they are the ones who give the AUthority.

Is this deceptive?

For me, it started deceptively with a few, more influential, people and now more of the general public are becoming increasingly aware of the notion of money – credit – debt and the illusion of it all. Because the knowledge is exposed, gaining momentum and spreading far-and-wide all across the world, the 'elite' cannot turn it around any longer. They have lost *all* control.

I know some people are fighting for their thousands, millions and billions to reclaim what was always theirs. But for me, it's not a fight. It's about exposing the TRUTH and shining the light on the dark side of the illusion of debt.

So, what happened to my ranch and my cattle as I represented myself in the courthouses?

Turn the page to find out.

"For a long time the New York Stock Exchange looked with suspicion on the investment trusts; only in 1929 was listing permitted."

~ John Kenneth Galbraith ~

10

Lost Property

"All crises have involved debt that, in one fashion or another, has become dangerously out of scale in relation to the underlying means of payment."

~ John Kenneth Galbraith - A Short History of Financial Euphoria ~

A system-less system.

That is how I see the Court of L.A.W.

It's filled with twists and turns that do not support the people.

LAW is 'Do No Harm' but the 'Legalities' are *harmful* and *threatening*.

In the course of my time in the 'Court of Queen's Bench', I had no lawyer, solicitor or barrister by my side aiding me. I chose this because of the high costs and also, I had no desire to be falsely represented by someone who only has one jurisdiction, which will only assist me if I'm *dead* or *lost at sea*!

It started with the process of giving an ex-partner a Second Mortgage and Private Property Security AGreement, rather than a wedding ring with a marriage contract. I originally owned a home with land, and when she moved in with me, she put some money into that property and so it became joint ownership.

Back then I did not have the knowledge that I know now and I could not speak the words in court, which were necessary to back myself up. But I quickly learned the truth of law along the way. I had nine sessions in court over a three year period and by the end, I felt strong enough and empowered to stand on my own as a sovereign, *living* man.

The judges would get so frustrated with me, as I would not adhere to their language and orders. I would repeatedly say, "I'm here! I'm alive! I don't know who you're talking about on that piece of paper". I would bumble my way through the proceedings but I often observed that the individual that sat up on the bench, would sigh or take deep breaths. It was obvious that they were pissed at me! At the end of my ninth attendance in court, the judge said to me "I've had enough. I don't know what to do with you, so go ahead to the Court of Appeals. You've won!"

But in the meantime, the process of selling my property was already in place.

All the way through that experience, I kept saying to the banks that the 1st mortgage had lines of credit before the 2nd mortgage. The 2nd mortgage was for my ex-partner, as the land was in my name. My first mortgage didn't back me up, as you will discover, as they would receive full funds and the bankers would hide behind my ex-partners skirt! Such trickery and deception from the banking world. Greed that you could not imagine.

My ex could have sold all of my properties and assets at a foreclosure rate, as people won't pay proper rates because the parasites prey on each other, ready to pounce and they would offer her way less than the 'true value'. But she opted not to do that. By the way, 'true value' is what I paid for it! As we all know, it's *MAN who creates* the value.

I tried to get the banks to join me in court "You guys all know the truth!" But they ignored me. I challenged lawyers on the phone "This is silly, you know I'm the creditor!" but it was useless and I would end the call "Go ahead and play your games". I know some of those guys were embarrassed because their job was on the line, so I sent them my sympathy.

So, when the sales happened, of course the value was less than what it should have been and this caused the first mortgage to completely take what was on their books; after I had paid *in excess* of one million dollars in interest, with my so-called 'principle' payments over decades. The second mortgage took the remainder of the fire sale of the land. And a private property security AGreement that I had also AUthorised with my female partner.

With the rest of the property, meaning my farming equipment, vehicles and machinery, I organised some of the sales because I wanted to try to protect my cow herd that I had built up after all of those years and in fact, some of those cattle are still in the hands of a man that is holding them for me, for when I wish to continue breeding them. They are pure bred cattle that are line bred, so this could give me an opportunity of starting the business again but for now, I am happy to know that I have this option. Line breeding is a lifetime process in selecting genetics to create the ultimate beef animal and I will share much more on this in the chapter *Bulldog Rancher*.

So, that judge said to me that I had won and for me to go to the Court of Appeal. I did as she stated. I went to the building and after talking with a woman at the desk, I realised that I had won no-thing! To even get through the door, you require $60,000 and the addition of all of my transcripts from nine attendances in court, which was an estimated $2,500 each and then you *have* to get a lawyer.

I looked at that lady as she gave me the list of rules and I said "It's okay dear, I understand. You're just here for your job. You're fully aware this place is empty because the people that come here, like me, have already had their money taken away from them, from the other people in court". I chuckled and left the building.

But I didn't stop there.

How could I?

This is me, Randall!

I had to prove *one* more thing to myself. So, I put together a document on my own, with all of the information that I had learnt about the 'system'. It basically said, foreign credit has no assets and I know you guys used my AUtograph paper to get credit but I'm the creditor and you wouldn't have anything if it wasn't for my *wet ink signature*, to make that PROMISE in the first place!

I phoned the bank to make an appointment to see them and respected their responses. "Oh yes, no problem. I'll get you a copy of that".

Me: I don't want a copy. I want the original wet ink signature document.

Over and over and over and over and finally this banker, Fred, said;

Fred: Well, come on into the office and we'll get this settled for you.

I arrived at the bank for our scheduled appointment.

Me: I have something that I want you to sign before we begin, are you able to do that for me?

Fred: All good. Come on in Randall.

We sat down.

Me: Do you mind signing this first before we start talking please? It says you can get me that wet ink signed document.

Fred: Oh yes, no problem.

He actually signed it in *black ink* and with that I knew he did not know what the fuck he was doing!

I won't go into too much depth about ink but the *WAY* you sign your name and the *colour ink* is <u>*very*</u> important. We are constantly told to sign in *black ink* which simply represents the strawman. When you receive any documents from the government or other attached organisations, your name is always in capital letters. Just take a look at your recent tax bills. Whether you call it your *property tax bill* or *council tax bill* or even if you check a letter from your bank, it will be in all capitals (e.g. RANDALL EARL KAISER). This is the strawman and in general, there is no signature from an individual, like a CEO or director, as they are all corporations.

My *ink* meanings are:
- Red = private man = HUMAN = living = blood of man
- Blue = statutory = artificial representation of the strawman
- Black = strawman = dead entity
- Green = assumed authority
- Purple = sovereign = Randall's favourite colour!

Look at all of the wonderful colours we have missed out on!

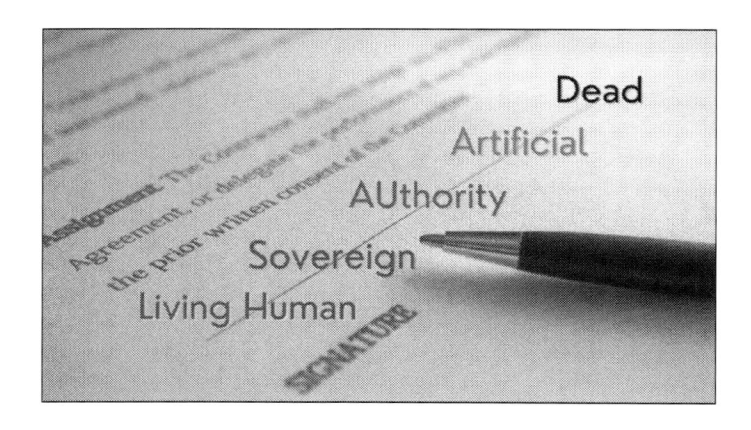

So, when this guy who had AUthority, signed this document, without understanding any of the details and putting his name in *black ink*. I smiled to myself!

Me: So, can you really get me the original?

Fred: I told you we can get a copy.

Me: No. You just signed a document that said that you can get me the original. So you're gonna have to do just that or admit that you did not understand anything that I have said to you. Otherwise, we're going to have to take this up with a lawyer.

Fred: Well, I'd better get my lawyer on the phone.

He did. The call turned into a conference call and the circles continued as before. I ask for the wet signature and they agree to a copy.

Me: You're not hearing me! Your man just signed a document that's in my hands, as we speak, which means that he agrees to get me those papers.

Lawyer: Well, we can't get you that.

Me: I know! But you said you could.

Lawyer: Can I talk to you in private, Fred?

With that, Fred leaves me in the room and takes the call from another office. When he returns, he simply escorts me out of the building saying "I can't talk to you anymore. You're going to have to leave."

Me: Fred, you know that I don't have any fucking money to take you to court and you also know that the fucking court protects you.

His eyes lowered and he could not make eye contact with me, he turned into a silent puppy.

The whole experience humoured me but don't get me wrong, I was angry and highly frustrated too, I'm not perfect.

What I do know is, that what I went through, many people have committed suicide with the stress, debt, loss of assets and feeling such despair and hopelessness. Some of those got so mind-fucked in the system-less system. And I simply, send them my love and I will never stop fighting for my freedom as a sovereign human living being. Sometimes I become a warrior and other times, I fight peacefully, with harmony and love.

I lost my property in the eyes of the Law but it's still there for me to reclaim, when I am ready. That cattle industry that I was in for decades, took me across the waters to China, to look for potential investors some years prior to me relinquishing my home. I wanted to play with the big boys in the larger corporations along the food chain industry and see what was in it for me!

"Wisdom, itself, is often an abstraction associated not with fact or reality but with the man who asserts it and the manner of its assertion."

~ John Kenneth Galbraith ~

11

Chinese Whispers

"The euphoric episode is protected and sustained by the will of those who are involved, in order to justify the circumstances that are making them rich. And it is equally protected by the will to ignore, exorcise, or condemn those who express doubts."

~ John Kenneth Galbraith - A Short History of Financial Euphoria ~

When we landed at Shanghai airport, I chuckled when I saw their welcome sign that was designed to greet the travellers.

"Welcome to China. Capitalism & Communism Working Hand in Hand."

I made the decision to visit China, with the main purpose of finding a business partner for a mega-beef project that I was proposing, knowing that I could create a good trade with my wisdom, my cattle that I loved and a ranch that I owned. I felt this was a brilliant opportunity to widen my scope and increase business and sales and to experience life outside of Canada. The investor would have the opportunity of being part of my enterprise and actually have an interest in my beef, rather than just selling the beef on my behalf.

Fuzhou is the capital district and one of the largest cities in the Fujian province in China, with seven million people plus twelve million in the surrounding areas. One man that we met in Fuzhou, was the 'Kingpin' of that city and I was surprised to find out that this man had a heart!   I assumed this guy would be a fierce and cold character but as we travelled in different areas of the city with his son, I saw another side to him and that he was actually a conscious and compassionate human being.

On our jaunt around, we stopped over in Beijing and I thought the people were beautiful, yet powerful. I was also intrigued at their way of doing business deals. It was like some tribal, cultural initiation. They had a way of getting the truth out of you, by getting you drunk! We had Pijiu / Píjiǔ beer and the hard liquor Baijiu, which can be as high as 60% proof in alcohol! Our meetings would begin by gathering together and as we sat down to eat our meal. We would discuss business proposals and engage in general conversation. Then the alcohol would be brought out, where we 'pounded' our way through it with speed and all that appeared to matter to the these business guys, was;

   - Who could drink the most?

   - Who could drink the fastest?

   - Who threw up first!

It was insane! But I did join in, even though I felt pretty uncomfortable with the speed and intensity of glugging so much booze, as it made no sense to me! We even arm-wrestled and enacted silly play fights, it was like "We have no weapons to harm you but we will beat you up if necessary!"

Business and Dining with Friends

I think that's why there are various types of martial arts in the Eastern world because weapons are illegal, unlike in the USA, Canada and other countries in the Western hemisphere. I feel this is much wiser as they use their mind, body and spiritual skills to master the art of combat, defence and peace.

In my mind, it felt odd to get drunk as a way of getting the truth out of someone. Madness! A bunch of boys playing stupid games but we did find conscious and awakened organic meat producers along the way, surprisingly!

My memory takes me back to one meeting in particular. We were eating an organic chicken dinner which was fabulous, with the addition of the drinking game! After a couple of hours of laughter, talks and a dizzy head, it was time to depart. When I got outside, I couldn't hold the food or booze in any longer and proceeded to give my gift to the pavement in the parking lot, it got the contents of my whole stomach! An English speaking guy made his way over to me, put his arm around my shoulder and slurred "You've won buddy!" I was pissed to the gills "I've won what?" The guy continued "He (the business man) puked already in the back seat of his car. You watch. Tomorrow morning he's going to be kissing your ass! You held your puke for the longest!" He was right. The other guy was all over us the next day!

I had translators present with me, as many of my connections in China did not speak English. I did find that when I travelled through, or via, Hong Kong though, there would be more possibilities of an easier interaction because there were more people speaking my native tongue! I was always intrigued how I only ever saw the local people on my walks around the city, from Tiananmen Square to the general markets and streets. I would question, "Where are all of the tourists, travellers and visitors from across

Tiananmen Square

the lands? Are there no other cultures that live amongst them?" These would be my thoughts as I ventured out daily and I knew that I certainly stood out with my height and my cowboy hat!

During one visit to a huge department store, I had an unexpected interaction with someone inside. With my limited lingo, I motioned to one guy who looked like he worked in the shop and showed him my camera. I gave him gestures, as best as I could, to show him that I wished to take some pictures of his meat stall. I assured him no faces or the stall holders would be on the images. He agreed as he was putting his own story together of my cowboy hat, the rancher side of me, cattle and beef. I took some shots and as I turned in another direction, I noticed a fish kiosk selling its wares and I raised my camera to take some more images and then all hell let loose!

I did not know what the hell I'd done? The man with the fish stall was literally screaming words at me that I didn't understand. He was flailing his arms in the air as he approached me, pointing at my camera. The thought, "Hey buddy, what up?" is what came out my mouth but in my mind it was like "Holy fuck buddy! What's up with you?" It was such a loud commotion, that another guy from another produce stall heard the drama and came over to see what was going on. He could tell that I did not speak the language and thankfully he knew some English "What are you doing?" he asked me. I told him that I had asked for permission to take some picture snaps of the display of foods. "Oh, okay." Then he turned to the fish man and explained it all. The eruption of emotions was because the fish stall holder was worried that I was trying to steal his prices and as a capitalist business owner, he thought that I was spying on him! Thankfully, it all settled down and we shook hands as the tensions evaporated with some smiles.

I had so many adventures on this land, it certainly has many memories for me that were entertaining and intense, all at the same time.

The streets of Fuzhou were wild and I held my breath on a few occasions!

"What do you mean by that, Randall?"

Well, it was everything that I did not expect. For example, the Min River is one of the largest rivers running through the Fujian province. When you walk past some parts of the canal that run through the city, you would know that you are walking past 'sewerage' because of the aroma in the air.

How are the sewers linked to the river?

Because the people of this city use the river to pee and poop in!

Yes, it's their toilet.

I tried to figure out how seven million people in the 21st century have no proper sanitation in their homes.

"How can people live like this?"

But they do.

When I took a walk out to the river, its colour was of a murky brown and grey hue and I thought "Well, this place gets a lot of rain here, so maybe that helps the cleaning process?" The water did not smell but if you approached or passed by a canal that was running into the river, then it was obvious what was coming through! The 'kingpin' even told me that he had his daily swim in this river!

But I'll tell you what will surprise you. These people are generally healthier than the ones that live in North America!

In this city, the government had taken it upon themselves to build apartments and many other buildings of duplexes and complexes with septic systems or something similar, for the people to move into. Millions and millions of $ and £'s had been pumped into creating something better for the people but the natives said no and chose to stay put in their shacks. So now, we have 'ghost towns' with no business, economy or a new way of life. Maybe it would have been better to have pumped that money into their current homes and cleaning systems, instead of trying to tell the people what is best for them and move them en masse elsewhere, from all they have ever known.

Crossing the streets of Fuzhou was also a time to brace yourself and dive in! One time, I was standing there watching an ox and cart moving along and a bus speeding past about ten times faster, with various cars whizzing by and all of the vehicles going in different directions, it was like a mad zoo! "How the hell am I gonna get across this street?" Puzzled as I was, a woman suddenly appeared by my side with a baby wrapped up and swaddled to her chest, and she just took off into the madness of the traffic! She weaved her way through like a professional and no one honked their horn or even slowed down to let her pass. "Holy shit! If she can do it, I can do it!"

So, I prepared myself… ready, steady, go!

I made it across the road!

The roads appear to have no rules or laws, well not according to the people I was travelling with!

Jason was a businessman that I spent time with and he showed me some of the delights of the land. Lisa was his personal assistant, translator and all other things to be in charge of his business when he was or was not in the country. Jason held her in high regard and valued her as a person and his employee. With that, he had purchased her a car and she would use this vehicle to transport us to places, meetings or for leisure. She was a sweet young thing and one day in busy traffic she was getting a little heated. "We have to get to this meeting, we cannot be late and the traffic is impossible. Can I go up on the sidewalk?" "Sure, whatever feels right" said Jason. Within seconds there with a big 'thump' as we were up on the pavement and here she was, navigating her way through the pedestrians! I was holding on tightly to whatever I could get a hold onto and then finally with another big 'thump', she put us safely back on the road. Unsure which one is safer, the sidewalk or the road!

One evening, when we had some time to enjoy ourselves away from business dealings, we made our way to a type of Disneyland for adults, which had various things for health and beauty.

I was amazed as we drove past some astounding mountains where I saw the mines, with large sections of holes and gaps to the front of this beautiful land. It was unbelievable! To reach our destination, we also had to drive through a tunnel that was about 6-8 kilometres long, before we landed in the car park. What I didn't realise, was that the entertainment had fifty different pools of water! From fish that nibble the toxins off your feet, to clays that cover your body and many other fun things. But, we had no swimwear! Jason and I were over six feet tall and the natives are much smaller in stature and all they could offer us, were their largest size that they had in swimming trunks but I called them the *'grapes of wrath'*!

The pants crushed certain delicate areas and disguised none of the other parts and we laughed! And we still had to cover ourselves up, going in and out of the waters, but it was fun.

I never said anything to Lisa about her driving skills, as she was happy with them. And leaving that car park with a, 'thump' 'thump' 'thump' over and over the speed bumps she would go "Why do they put these stupid things here?". "To slow you down" I said. But her comments did make some sense because there was no traffic, no cars and yet there were all of these speed bumps. Once again, I was astounded at the magnitude of these places, which had been built with humongous parking lots that were basically empty! The money used from the economy, which is ultimately the people's money, was being spent on things that the general local person could not afford and there were so few visitors from around the world.

Where is the sense in this?

It was not all roads and bumps though. Lisa had escorted us to open areas of land with miles and miles of greenhouses growing various produce. During our tour, I saw a mountain coming right out of the ground! Now it may not sound odd to you but it was such a strange vision because the land was flat for miles and then there was this 'thing' sticking up out of the ground. It reminded me of a type of ancient pyramid and I wondered if it was a man-made structure. How could it be there? It looked so accidental but entrancing too! It had been there so long that the trees, shrubs and plants had made their home there. At the top of the mountain sat a wooden structure with railings around it. It looked about five storeys high and it was all rickety. In awe, I said to Lisa and Jason, "I wanna go up there.", and only Lisa decided to join me in this experience.

We made our way up the stairwell and looked out at the spectacular and breath-taking views, from the railings. We were then approached by a monk, who appeared to be Buddhist or Taoist but a beautiful man, who asked us both if we wished to enter the Temple inside "Hell yeah!" was my response but Lisa declined. This gentle man took my hand and held it like I was his new best friend! He directed

Forbidden City Temple of Heaven

me into this Temple and he knelt us both down by the incense and the other monks, as we prayed together⋯to whom? Well, that's what doesn't matter because it's all one, whomever you believe in because it comes from the heart and when you can be in this reverence of peace, harmony and love, then all feels serene in one's soul⋯it was a deeply touching experience.

Beautiful People and Ceremonies

The food had its own delicacies and there were times that Jason took me out in the evening for a beer and some 'street meat'. The first time we went out together, he said to me "It's up to you what you eat but I won't eat anything unless it's got wings!" I now know what the other 'chunks' of meat were. They could be anything from snake, dog, rat, maggots and whatever is available to the business stall holder, which actually could be a positive thing if you turn it around on itself. It's making use of what you can eat for sustenance and all of the various parts from the intestines to the ears, for business, trade and food. In truth, it's good to use the whole animal but in the Western world, this has been manipulated into believing that it's an apparently disgusting thing to do and when we do see these other countries and their food source, with what they choose to eat, we may be offended or disgusted at their attitude. But I see things differently. I know I am sharing my experiences in a jovial way but whatever food you are brought up with, then that's what you eat, as it's commonplace for you and your family and traditional to eat it. Offal and chicken feet, as an example, are delicious and true delicacies. I certainly would recommend societies and individuals look deeper into the production and creation of their food and learn where it's coming from.

Is it via the multinational corporations?

Do you know how it is actually formed, made and its origination from its humble beginnings?

How does it reach the end product that you see on the shelves in the stores and shops that you purchase from?

Maybe open your mind to the possibility, that the people eating food in a way that repels you may be a more beneficial approach to consuming

Organic Pork & Chicken Farmer Retail Store

nourishment for one's overall health.

I did, however, ensure that I trusted my gut-instincts when ordering my 'street meat!' I enjoyed the food each time and had no illness or digestive upsets. I'm still here!

I will share one final story on dining in China.

Organic Farmer Retail store –
Pork and Chicken

We were cordially invited by some officials to join them for dinner. As we travelled to an oceanfront Restaurant for our evening meal, we had the privilege of having a Police escort vehicle in front of us, which parted the traffic ahead of us so that we could drive through the streets without any delays. The food was nothing spectacular, just nice enough and we were treated like royalty. Then it was time to leave and we were greeted by the owners of the eating house. We had polite conversation as the proprietor asked if we enjoyed our meal and this guy was thrilled to share with us that his food was always fresh and locally produced, including the fish that was freshly caught that morning straight from the river. Thankfully, I did not react in front of him, as I remembered the apparent, seven million people that use the river as a toilet!

I will highlight though, that the 'MainStream Media' (MSM) dispels the truth of what goes on with our neighbouring countries, tribes and cultures and promotes fear of strangers or tries to portray that what these other people are doing is 'bad', compared to our lifestyle choices.

Thankfully, I see the goodness in the people and what's in their credit systems and their organic food production.

I was told that there were an estimated 1.3 billion people in China.

Are there?

I shared with you the estimated population but all I saw was the ghost cities that had been built for the people, yet remained empty. There was so much land dedicated to industrial parks and import duty-free zones, which were still being built. All I could see was acres and acres of roads, trees, empty buildings and parking lots. I had been on the road for hours at a time and it was desolate! This was not simply from driving in a car around a few cities but I saw exactly the same thing when I was travelling between Beijing-Shanghai on the Bullet Train.

Now this is one amazing experience to have!

I had no idea what to expect, as I watched the speedometer at the front of the train that was in view, as I chatted with my companions. I saw it start at 30 km/h and then rise to 60 km/h in a short space of time. I continued talking and at one point, my eyes caught the speed going at 300 km/h! We were standing up and I never felt any change from leaving the station to reaching such a high speed, it was phenomenal! When you are seated on an aeroplane, you are immersed in the take-off, lift-off and with the additional landing experience but with this train, it's an advanced technological communication system that has no contact with the rail, it's levitating! The Bullet Train can reach a top speed of 350 km/h which is 217 mph.

High Level American Lady Banker and an Advisor to President Duterte

One of my travelling buddies was a pipe contractor and he was buying pipes from places similar to China, to bring back to Canada. His company had bought a plant and some land in one of these industrial estates and on the developed streets. There were huge facilities in the middle of nowhere. Some projects were anywhere up to $650 billion or as high as a trillion dollars and one of those designs was to create an infrastructure of roads from China through to Pakistan. Yes, it was another amazing idea to build some base structure but at what cost? As things go, it's the next step of slavery by cause of the Chinese Communist Party (CCP), that have their 'fingers' in everything! All projects are with the government, so they gather the people to work for them.

The pyramid of exploitation becomes evident when you dive deeper into these experiences. The majority of the general public do not have a clue what is behind the closed doors of these types of organisations and corporations. The 'elite' convince the people that they know what is best to establish order and lifestyle, which is a complete psychological operation. As an example, if you look at the current day lockdown from the coronavirus, it's a procedure with an agenda. I consider this plan to be in the midst of a war as both players, you may want to call it the good guys and the bad guys, are battling it out.

Unfortunately, we were never able to get an investment on-board my project. We did have Memorandums of Understanding (MOU) signed and just one MOU, has paperwork that is inches thick. I took several of these back with me to Canada with the hope of showing these documents to a bank with the desired outcome, which was to receive a loan for my project. But sadly, no bank would take us on with the fear of doing any deals with China or having any faith or trust in them.

Yellow Dragon Family Front Man

Looking back now, it's so obvious to me that the banks were the 'gatekeepers', being the globalist multinational companies. They had it all and these banks chose not to take on my ideas, vision or projects, because it doesn't make **them** the money or create and stabilise **their** leadership in the marketplace.

It always re-establishes itself back to that Pyramid of Exploitation.

"The man who is admired for the ingenuity of his larceny is almost always rediscovering some earlier form of fraud. The basic forms are all known and have all been practiced. The manners of capitalism improve. The morals may not."

~ John Kenneth Galbraith ~

12

The Pyramid of Exploitation

"Faced with the choice between changing one's mind and proving that there is no need to do so, almost everybody gets busy on the proof."
~ *John Kenneth Galbraith* ~

The Global Pandemic has uprooted the Whole World.

Upside Down or the Right Way Up?

In an earlier chapter, I told you that I was thrown off my YouTube channel for the first time when I shared my thoughts and ideas on the clear data and facts, which I had researched. All the information in the public domain of the MSM did not support what the government was telling its people. I believed the number of people dying of 'coronavirus cases' was no bigger or greater than any other year previous, compared to the seasonal flu death numbers. Now a seasonal flu is not necessarily the killer of a person but if that human has other underlying health issues in whatever way, this is how they will generally die because their physical system does not have the strength to defend the body and attack the enemy, let's call this enemy the *virus*.

Now, what is a virus?

Almost every ecosystem on Earth contains viruses. Simply put, WE would not exist if our human form did not contain viruses. This has been the same since time began and will continue to be like this, for as long as this Earth exists. A virus is a genetic material, either in the formation of our DNA or an RNA. Viruses evolve constantly due to our surroundings and experiences because our human form is physical, emotional, mental and energetic to what we can see *and* what we cannot see, with the naked eye. Now, I'm not here to give you a major scientific lesson or intricate details but what I'm here to remind you of, is that your atoms and cells are designed naturally to know what to do if an enemy strikes, that being an *alien* virus, bacteria or particle. By alien, I mean incompatible, conflicting or separate, not the ones in spaceships!

Your humanness responds with a variety of ways to remove this alien invader, through the natural elements found inside the body's internal systems. Water, fire, earth, air and spirit. That's what you're made up of and this began in your mother's womb when you went from a cell to an embryo, to the magical creation of the wonders of this universe, which in turn created you, that beautiful baby!

I'm not a disease specialist but John is. John Ioannidis from Stanford University, who is apparently one of the greatest specialists of diseases from around the world, declared in August 2020:

"It's not the Plague, it's not even the flu. For the sake of modern civilization itself, we have to forget all about COVID-19."

In October 2020 he cited:

"3.4% is the given rate from the World Health Organization (WHO) that has caused horror and is meaningless⋯For a healthy person under the age of 70 only ONE in 2,000 will die which is a mere 0.05% of the population."

So, if this virus is nothing more than a general flu season, then something larger is afoot!

Dr. Michael Yeadon who is a former Vice President & CSO at Pfizer has clearly *stated "I am warning you⋯your government is lying to you in ways that are easy for you to establish. If you choose not to do that, there is nothing that someone like me can do about that. You have been subject to propaganda and lies by people who are very well trained in how they do that."*

- Mandatory masks are insidious psychological weapons.
- Forced isolation is demeaning our human rights and our dignity.
- PCR tests are a false methodology based on a computer virus and not a human virus.
- Vaccines that were intended to become your passport to life, are the work of the 'elite'.

The **false** narrative told us that there was a deadly novel virus sweeping the planet. Not one person is immune to it and there is no cure. Asymptomatic people are major drivers of the disease, so we have to lock down *everyone* and you must *all* wear masks until *every* person is vaccinated. Anyone who challenges this narrative is a danger to society.

The **reality** is that few people are susceptible to severe disease. There are several treatments available, if someone has a disease. The asymptomatic people are *not* the major drivers of disease. Lockdown and mask mandates do *not* work and cause great *harm* to the people and in our societies, as a whole. The vulnerable were hurt and damaged along the course of these actions that were implemented, which did *not* help the vulnerable human being, in any way, shape or form.

So, what are the governments doing?
Who are they listening to?
What advice are they taking?
What agenda do they have for the people?

BUILD BACK BETTER

Do you recognise this expression?

It is currently being used by specific governments to manipulate the minds of the people.

'The Great Reset' ~ 'One World Order' ~ 'New World Order'

The effort put into this agenda, plan, scheme or programme, has been going on way before WWII. And the RMS Titanic was not just a film script with Leonardo de Caprio and Kate Winslet.

It was a great historical reminder to the people, that if you do not follow the rules of the 'elite', you will go down and drown no matter your regal title, official status or as a peasant under the decks.

RMS Titanic

It may sound like I have jumped off course from the virus but I haven't as it's all inter-linked.

Have you ever wondered why the Titanic became so famous?

Has no other passenger liner ever capsized?

In one hundred years, there must have been other transatlantic liners, which have plummeted to the depths of the seas?

But none of them are remembered as much as RMS Titanic.

The Titanic is a reminder, to obey or wither and die.

RMS Titanic sank in the North Atlantic Ocean on 15th April 1912.

The Titanic purposely attracted highly influential people and bloodlines that were specifically chosen because they *disagreed* with the idea of the Federal Reserve. Once the people had been taken out of the equation, then the 'elite' could proceed forthwith and The Federal Reserve Act was created on 23rd December 1913.

These patterns were designed with a purpose.

The tactics were masterly and skilful.

And it continued with a *drip-feed* strategy, which was filtered out to the general public on a daily, weekly, monthly and annual basis, decade after decade after decade. This was to test and trial the people to see how far an innocent human being would easily and unwittingly give up their *free-will*, without receiving full disclosure, as they adhere to the trust of the 'chosen' leaders.

>What are YOU willing to accept in your life?

>What are YOU willing to accept in your home?

>What are YOU willing to accept in your street?

>What are YOU willing to accept in your community?

>What are YOU willing to accept in your society?

What are YOU willing to accept in your culture?

What do YOU say '*no* more' to?

What will YOU refuse from these echelons?

The 'elite' forced us to play a serious game of chess, with an outcome that only suited their agenda. But a chess game has an opponent and it's only a matter of time, where the arrogant player who has won so many times with deception, trickery and illusions of their own faith, that they put less and less energy into strategy because the player believes he/she has won the game, even before the first chess piece is handled. But I would call that laziness and never, ever underestimate the opposition!

Eventually the smug and pretentious player suddenly realizes they have finally lost the game and can never return to play again, with a human soul.

> You are here now.
>
> It is our time.
>
> To *Re*-Build the *Re*-Public.

We do not consent to false wars, division or separation of us the people, through religious beliefs, hypocrisy, duality, sexual seclusion and untruths that were unjust.

ALL crimes against humanity are now ceased and any individual will be tried for treason, bio-terrorism and economic sabotage via The

Nuremberg Code created for the people in 1947 to put a stop to unethical human experimentation from WWII. Justice will be done on Earth.

It was the evil intentions of the 'elite' and the trapped souls within the bloodlines who were cornered and unable to leave their families, that was the cause of inhumane experimentation on the human soul.

They are the virus.

They are the enemy.

They are a foreign entity that cannot co-exist with a loving human.

Their value to experiment, was purely from narcissistic behaviour.

Experimentation is everywhere because there is *value* in it.

The value comes from what you want to gain from the experiment.

What you want to gain comes from your ego, during the experiment.

Your ego attributes to a positive or negative intention on the experiment.

I believe we *all* experiment in some way, during the course of our lives.

That is how we find balance in ourselves.

We all have been unloving or unkind or much worse! But salvation comes from within. At some point, every one of us has:

- Analyse
- Prove

- Research
- Probe
- Examine
- Sample
- Speculate
- Study
- Verify
- Practise
- Try out
- Messed around with
- Put something or someone to the test

An experiment is in the hands of the individual and then can expand into families, tribes and culture.

I believe EGO = being HUMAN.

Maybe being human is one lifelong experiment with ourselves and with others?

A human being can be kind or unkind.

A human being can be loving or unloving.

A human being can be true or false.

So, as a human being, and this includes members of the 'elite', you still get to choose how you wish to live your life through your relations and relationships. Relationships are not just with another person but with everything.

Your relationship with your parents/guardians/elders.

Your relationship with your siblings and cousins.

Your relationship with your child/children and grandchild/children.

Your relationship with your friends and partnerships.

Your relationship with your marriage or unity of another.

Your relationship with your colleagues at work or in business.

Your relationship with your lifestyle choices.

Your relationship with your personal health.

Your relationship with your personal finances.

Your relationship with your beliefs and morals.

Your relationship with your governments and leaders.

Your relationship with every single person you have ever known.

Your relationship with every single person you will ever meet.

Your relationship with yourself.

With the variety of options that I listed earlier on ways we *'experiment'* in our relations and relationships, I believe we all use these options often.

I suppose, that's what the 'elite' did, manipulating relationships to suit a personal outcome and I know of a well-used term and phrase, circulating in our modern society as narcissist – narcissistic - narcissism. This usually stands for;

Ego-tism
Ego-ist
Ego-centric
Ego-mania

I would call this type of ego coming from a negative place.

Ego can be love.

It just depends on how your mind and heart work together or separately and that's what delivers an outcome.

If you feel confused about any of this, then you will have to dig a little deeper into your conscience and try to figure this out.

I am not attacking the 'elite'. I am not supporting the 'elite'. I am making you aware of the 'elite'. So if I'm looking at both sides of the coin, then it expands the brain. A bit like standing on the top of Nose Hill Park and having the full 360° panoramic view. Then you get to choose which direction you wish to walk in.

I experimented with value in my business on the ranch, which led me through a chain of events before I lost my property.

"In all life one should comfort the afflicted, but verily, also, one should afflict the comfortable, and especially when they are comfortably, contentedly, even happily wrong."

~ John Kenneth Galbraith ~

13
The Retail 'Value' Chain

"Faced with the choice between changing one's mind and proving that there is no need to do so, almost everybody gets busy on the proof."
~ John Kenneth Galbraith ~

Since the 1960's and 70's, the cattle industry and other food trade productions, were moving away from conventional to unconventional methods. Instigated by the 'leaders'.

My ranching business became one of the first retro-pioneers in my city, opting for change in the industry, with the desire to return to the traditional formulas.

I had some great ideas and we, as a team, were able to reboot the 'laws of beef' and restore the 'old ways' of ranching. During my first decade in this industry, we learned how to grow certain breeds and types of animals and learned how to naturally modify them, rather than using chemicals. Our consideration was what was best for the greater whole, from the animal to human. This included our lands of pasture and for it be a place called home, for our animals. It was all about the value chain. This was our promotion from 'Pasture-to-Plate'. Totally natural.

Then Mad Cow Disease - *bovine spongiform encephalopathy* (BSE) hit the beef crisis in Canada.

On the 20th May 2003, the Canadian Food Inspection Agency announced that a Black Angus cow, from northern Alberta has been found to have BSE. The United States immediately closed its border to Canadian beef and cattle. About 40 countries followed suit.

I just knew something 'screwy' was going on here. Seriously!

My mind was open to the idea that something was amiss. Because the price of beef did NOT drop and the price of the carcass in a box from our Canadian plants, to the buyers in the U.S. did NOT drop but the price of cattle plummeted!

It was only 15 years previously that *Cargill* and *Tyson* foods came into Canada. These two huge companies decided to take the land and build their plants, which the government fully supported but sadly wiped out all of the smaller packers and slaughterhouses in the process.

Cargill Limited is now one of Canada's largest merchandisers and processors. Which includes the processing of beef, poultry and oilseed, and the manufacturing of livestock feed. In addition, they are involved in crop input product retailing, as well as grain handling, milling, salt distribution and merchandising. Cargill is managed by the fourth richest billionaire family in the United States - the Cargill-MacMillan family.

Tyson Foods Canada Inc. produces and distributes food products. The Company offers breads, patties, lunch sandwiches, sliced meats, sausages, desserts, chicken, and bakery products. Tyson is owned by Bloomberg.

Back in those days, my attitude was "Fuck you Cargill! I'll spend the rest of my life kicking your ass outta my country!" It was hard for my brain to understand what was happening as I watched it destroy my industry and I observed my fellow ranchers go down around me. This was difficult for me to watch, as I'd witnessed grown men close down their plants and I got to see glimpses of their souls being ripped out, it was so sad.

The land that was used for raising the cattle, became barren and there was not enough profit at that lower level. Many of the farmers tried a BSE action classed lawsuit but some of them, eighteen years on, are still ongoing.

This is because of the Admiralty/Maritime Judicial Law, where the 'system' protects the multinational corporations and **_not_** the smaller businesses.

Our business was decimated too. We had gone from 100,000 beef cattle producers down to 40,000 producers.

BSE first appeared in the 1980s in the United Kingdom.

"There remains no scientific proof that BSE can be transmitted to man by beef" British Health Secretary Stephen Dorrell, told the House of Commons.

British officials insisted that scientists will likely have to study the disease for at least two more years before they can determine definitively whether the disease can be transmitted to humans from cattle.

Over two decades, during 1980's and 90's, over **four million** heads of cattle were slaughtered in an effort to contain the outbreak, and *ONLY* **177** people died after contracting the Variant Creutzfeldt–Jakob Disease (vCJD/CJD) by **allegedly**, eating infected beef.

Did you calculate that?

So, in 20 years, only 177 people **allegedly** died and 4,000,000 cattle were slaughtered.

So, where's the crisis?

A crisis that killed hundreds, if not thousands, of small agricultural and local farming businesses. But the corporations became multinational and are multi-billionaires.

Where did the panic originate from?

During this time, a British buddy came into the picture, Mark Purdy. The author of 'Animal Pharm: One Man's Struggle to Discover the Truth About Mad Cow Disease and Variant CJD'.

This is an overview of the book:

'Mark Purdey's life changed one day in 1984 when a Ministry of Agriculture inspector told him he must administer a toxic

organophosphate pesticide to his dairy herd. Passionately committed to organic farming and convinced of the harmful effects of chemicals in the environment, he refused to comply. 'It was as if my whole life became focused', he explained later. Before they had a chance to prosecute, Purdey took the Ministry to court and won his case. These experiences led him to challenge the orthodox line on the origins of Mad Cow Disease and its human counterpart variant CJD. Could the insecticide used in the official programme have precipitated the spread of the disease?

Purdey's quest to discover the truth was hampered at every turn by government bureaucracies and self-serving scientific cliques who sought to smear and marginalize him. Dogged by dirty tricks and forced to work alone as something of a scientific sleuth, he struggled to reveal hidden interests and dangerous secrets.

Increasingly skeptical of the official narrative, Purdey was certain that toxic environmental factors would provide answers, and so embarked on a self-funded worldwide odyssey to investigate. 'Animal Pharm' follows him on these eco-detective trails to locations as diverse as Iceland, Sardinia, Colorado and Australia. Purdey uncovers contamination from industry, munitions, pesticides, nuclear experiments and natural geology, linking these with the emergence of a range of neurodegenerative diseases. His research is at once compelling and disturbing, helping to create a paradigm shift in our understanding of the relationship of pollutants to disease and health'.

When Mark and I were in contact, he shared with me his studies on the UK outbreak. He told me that the **prion** protein is actually naturally occurring in our bodies and especially concentrated in our brain and our central nervous system.

> Me: What is the prion protein for?
>
> Mark: To get rid of heavy metals. So, specific prion proteins will attach themselves to the metals to remove them, as an alien entity.
>
> Me: So, the prions are not the problem?
>
> Mark: No, it's the **overload** of metals that's the problem! If there's too much metal, the prion cannot do its job by going through the interstitial fluid, back into the blood to get rid of it and when the metals breaches the blood-brain barrier or the central nervous system, it becomes even harder because they are only meant to do that work, at a microscopic level.
>
> Me: But when there is so much metal, how does it go back out of the blood-brain barrier?

Mark: It can't! So, it misfolds as the prion *over collects* and now it has all of these metals heavily attached to it, where it ends up forming a *crystal* and then it gets to the point that the animal can go whacky!

Me: What causes the animal to go whacky?

Mark: *Sound*!

The misfolded crystallised prion will react with such sensitivity e.g. sonic booms from aircrafts or military air force bases. You can literally see the animals' sudden reaction with their heads and their bodies and some would even fall to the ground. Some of the animals would go completely bananas! Because their brain could explode from the crystals exploding in the brain!

Mark was a dear friend and taught me a lot about animals.

The cattle are animals and so are we! We are mammals.

The prions exist in our brains too.

So, what do you think the metals are and where do they come from?

The modern phrase we use is '*heavy metals*' and that is true.

The metals are a *metallic* element, which is toxic and has a high density, specific gravity or atomic weight. With metal being an alien entity, the body is doing its best to rid of it.

The toxic metals that the body is attempting to *dump* out of the the physical system are:

- Cobalt
- Chromium
- Lithium
- Iron
- Copper
- Aluminium
- Mercury
- Arsenic
- Cadmium

Heavy metals are naturally occurring elements that have a high atomic weight and a density at least five times greater, than that of water.

This is our modern age because of multiple industrial, domestic, agricultural, medical and technological applications which have led to their wide distribution in the environment, meaning the multinational organisations.

This is of great concern to our human health and its problems and the damage created to our environment.

These metals create our diseases.

- Cancer
- Leukaemia
- Tumours

- Children's diseases
- Alzheimer's
- Dementia
- Schizophrenia
- Bipolar
- Depression
- Arthritis
- Asthma
- Chronic Fatigue Syndrome
- Organ Diseases
- Anxiety
- Autism
- ADHD
- Diabetes
- Hormone Imbalances
- Acne/psoriasis/eczema
- ...the list is endless!

These metals drip feed their way into our physical systems on a miniscule level and over time, they become long-term disabilities or ailments.

Why would our governments allow this to happen to us?

Why would our leaders allow this?

Why would these corporations allow this?

In our environments

In our water

In our food

In our medication

In the air we breathe!

The metals are everywhere and this has shortened our life span. The false historic data like Wikipedia, that gets edits and revised over and over, gives us misinformation. As humans, we should be living to over a hundred years of age and in a state of wellness, without all of those physical, mental and emotional issues. There is *natural* degeneration of the human form and then there is *forced* degeneration, which deteriorates your atoms and cells too fast. You can find this information via various methods, such as ancient scrolls and scribes, wall carvings and symbology.

What is the truth?

Just because it's not *your* truth, does not make it untrue.

Just because the *majority* follow something, does not mean it's the *right, good or best* way.

Life has endless questions and you have your whole life to get the answers!

I did all that I could to educate others with my knowledge and wisdom and this even took me into the political arena, as I tried to get my messages out to the everyday Rancher.

"The world of finance hails the invention of the wheel over and over again, often in a slightly more unstable version. All financial innovation involves, in one form or another, the creation of debt secured in greater or lesser adequacy by real assets."

~ John Kenneth Galbraith ~ A Short History of Financial Euphoria ~

14

Bulldog Rancher

"More die in the United States of too much food than of too little"
~ John Kenneth Galbraith ~

I was a Bovine Genetic Engineer!

How's that for a cowboy rancher!

I loved my profession and I was very passionate about my cattle and land in keeping everything as natural as possible. I discovered every aspect of the cattle industry, over three decades. From thinking about making the cows to removing the eggs from cows, adding sperm and then putting the eggs back into the cows. I would dig into every arena of cattle ranching, as I was intrigued with the whole process of pasture-to-plate. It was never about how wealthy I could be but for the love of purebred food from a beautiful beast, which gives nourishment to the people.

In my early twenties, during my first few naïve years in the industry, I was the typical kinda rancher. I would use fertilizer on my hay crops with the addition of using hormone growth 'promotants' on my cattle. "What am I using this shit for?" I found myself saying.

I had got to the point in my business, when I was told to use additives here and there and there and here, it was crazy and nonsensical. The excuse of 'lack' to back the idea of chemical, commercial farming and ranching made no sense to me, "We could feed the population of Japan with food grown in the ditches of my amazing expansive Alberta province in Canada."

I started to get 'black-bulled' in my trade because I was asking questions.

In my mind, I knew that the hormonal growth promotant implants that have been used since the 1950's, which are approved by the Food and Drug Administration (FDA), were simply being promoted to the farmers and ranchers, for sales and profit. I'm not just talking about my animals but these chemicals and toxins are in a lot of our food sources. Back then I only saw it first hand in North America but I knew that Europe and China had different standards and I wanted to know why? These were simple questions to ask.

"Why were the European and Chinese standards higher than the United States or Canada?"

They refused to accept our business because of the growth hormone enhancers i.e. promotants that are used to gain weight. "So, how come it's alright to sell this lower standard of meat, to our people, in our provinces and states?"

If I shared my thoughts with Canadians, they would say "Oh, that's ridiculous!"

If I shared my thoughts with Europe/China, they would say "Yes, you're right!"

I mentioned earlier that I'd got into the political arena, trying to get my message out to the everyday rancher. I was actually delegated as a candidate and was just off winning my seat on the Board of Directors by just 'six' votes! But I was running on one platform and one platform only and that was "If we have BSE, we have the option to examine the animal and find out if it's sick or not. We can use some kind of test for BSE on the animals and use those results as a sales technique i.e. we will guarantee non-infected animals.

I was trying to educate the people over round table meetings and I even got the opportunity to have a microphone in my hand once in a while ...but as you can imagine, it would be cut short or they would turn the volume off!

That's a joke, they didn't. But I bet they wished they could have done it!

My words were the TRUTH. But everything I said was looked upon as a bad idea because the average guy would not make profit, especially the feedlot producers.

What's a feedlot?

A feedlot is a type of animal feeding operation which is used in intensive animal farming, notably beef cattle, but also swine, horses, sheep, turkeys, chickens or ducks, prior to slaughter. The basic principle of the feedlot is to increase the amount of fat gained by each animal as quickly as possible; if animals are kept in confined quarters rather than being allowed to range freely over grassland, they will gain weight more quickly and efficiently, with the added benefit of economies of scale.

What's **in** a feedlot?

A mixture of corn, corn by-products (some of which is derived from ethanol and high fructose corn syrup production), milo, barley, and various grains such as wheat, barley, maize and oat. Some rations may also contain roughage such as corn stalks, straw, sorghum, or other hay, cottonseed meal, antibiotics, fermentation products, micro & macro minerals and even a drug can be added into a farm's feed, if required by a vet. Chickpeas (garbanzo beans), and occasionally potatoes are used as feed. Sadly, a lot of feedlot is also from artificially grown grains. Because once again, these organisations and governments interfered with the people's lands. For example; wheat.

Remember the days when you ate a hot dog and the bread was so natural?

I do!

But now the industry has shaped and de-formed the crops. These corporations told us the people that wheat was bad for our bodies and then a man-made title was created as gluten.

Is 'gluten' harmful to us?

The industry wished to reduce this gluten for us, to help us···how kind!

The answer, they believed, was to spray the wheat with glyphosate.

What is glyphosate?

It's a herbicide.

What's herbicide?

Herbicide is commonly known as a weed killer!

But the wheat is not a weed, so why do you want to kill it?

The truth about glyphosate, is that it does not just kill plants, it explodes them! That's right, EXPLODES them!

Glyphosate is not the poison itself but the *action* and *reaction* it enacts on the wheat.

It is believed that if the wheat explodes, then the good bacteria will create more food and have the ability to harvest it faster. It's a lie!

Because when the wheat explodes, the good bacteria dies!

The bacteria is growing at such a fast unnatural rate, that when the wheat explodes it loses its enzymes and its complete life force energy which is desecrated.

So, simply gluten-free is not healthy, it's artificial!

Have you ever read the ingredients on the packaging?

I am sure there are ten plus elements all mixed up and combined. Generally, the ingredients are 'glue'. Not the glue that you stick things together with in creative arts or broken objects, but in essence, it's the same. Depending on the brand, there can be starches, flours, sweeteners, guar gum to mimic bread but it's not real bread. If you research the ingredients, it's a science project!

Sadly, when you purchase bread or a 'loaf' off the shelves, it's not high in price for a reason. Because they are not using pure grain flour. They will use things **similar** e.g. fortified wheat flour.

What is fortified wheat flour?

By statute any white wheat flour that is milled, apparently has to have calcium carbonate, iron, thiamine/Vitamin B1 and Nicotinic acid added.

After the war, the government decided that white wheat flour needed the same vitamins as wholemeal flour. For over 60 years this has been added to the flour.

But why do we need to **add** something to Mother Nature?

She knows exactly what she's doing!

It's the food industries that turn our natural produce sour and create an altered state because of man and his experiments! We are constantly being experimented on! And if all of these foods were truly healthy, why is there so much disease in our current times? As a species of humans, we have never been so unwell! We keep taking supplements and extra additions to our fruit, vegetable, meat and dairy.

Why?

That has become another industry in itself!

I will offer a suggestion with this theme of wheat.

Research for an ethical supplier. Hopefully you have access to this in your country. Even give them a call and speak with them to ask some details that I have shared with you. If you feel it resonates with you, then order some flour, purchase some yeast and then create a loaf of bread. You may make some errors but find the fun in its creation and then see how your physical body reacts to that loaf of bread, obviously don't eat the whole loaf at once!

So what's the difference between conventional and nonconventional beef raised in a traditional fashion?

Let's start with the **conventional** method.

This conventional diet, is intended to weight gain in a short period of time. Cattle in those feedlots are fed grain rather than more natural forage. The desired outcome is for the animals' to gain an additional 400-600 pounds (180 kg) during its approximate 200 days in the feedlot, depending on its entrance weight into the lot, and also how well the animal gains muscle. Once the cattle are fattened up to their finished weight, the fed cattle are transported to a slaughterhouse.

The cattle industry works in sequence with one another. Prior to entering a feedlot, young calves are born typically in the spring where they spend the summer with their mothers in a pasture or on rangeland. Once the young calves reach a weight between 300-700 pounds (140 -320 kg) they are rounded up and either sold directly to feedlots, or sent to cattle auctions for feedlots to bid on them. Once transferred to a feedlot, they are housed and looked after for the next six to eight months where they are fed a mixed ration.

In my little story this 'feedlot' process begins with the '3-R's'.

    1. RALGRO

    This is a testosterone replacement, anabolic agent/anabolic steroid.

So, when the calves are young, the females are not physically interfered with but the males have their balls removed which is apparently, to calm them down. They then become fatter, rather than muscular. Testosterone generally promotes muscle as a natural process and thus the replacement tries to balance out the growth of that animal, to get some more muscle into the animal, as well as its laziness to gain fat which is brought in with this anabolic steroid. There are numerous brands on the market but Ralgro is the most notorious. The anabolic steroid comes in the form of a pellet and this is directly inserted into the outer part of the ear because it's the easiest place to put it into. Some ranchers do put the pellet in the gut but in general, it's inserted into the outer ear.

Now, if you insert something into the skin, the body will think this is an alien invasion and go for the attack. It's the enemy, as we have discussed before. It's a natural reaction from the physical form to protect itself from the abnormal organism, in this case, a 'pellet implant'. It's an instinctive and reasonable reaction for interrupting the natural mechanics of a mammal!

Now, because of this invasion another addition is now needed on top of the steroid, which is a slow releasing antibiotic. This double action is Ralgro.

Why give this antibiotic to the animal?

Because if you don't, its frickin ear will fall off! Because you have forced something foreign into the skin of the ear of an animal.

Why can we not let the animal find its own balance naturally?

Profit and Sales!

2. RACTOPAMINE HYDROCHLORIDE

Promotes the expansion of muscle tissue to retain water.

- Stimulation

It stimulates the animal and gets them excited.

Why do you want to stimulate an animal?

Stimulating the animal can create other challenges (e.g. unsettled in their setting or they become over-excitable). This is intense when they are going to the slaughterhouse, they are ramming from side to side through the walkways of fencing. There is also a phrase in the cattle industry termed as the 'dark-cutters'. This is when no blood comes out of the animal because of tension in the muscles from the stimulants.

- Feed additive

It is put into the feed to promote water retention so that the muscle tissue becomes spacious. This 'space' surrounds the atoms and molecules to hold water. Cells are filled with water too.

So for the last days of this animal's life, the muscle tissue expands thus promoting water retention.

For what reason?

Weight!

Because meat is sold by the pound.

*These drugs have even been used on children for asthma! If the lungs are dry, this stimulates and expands the space in the organ. The muscle tissue can then retain more moisture to hydrate the breath.

As of 2014, the use of Ractopamine Hydrochloride was banned in 160 countries and is still in debate today as it is illegal for humans, unless prescribed.

3. RUMENSIN

The main purpose of this ingredient is to kill bacteria in the rumen. The rumen is the first chamber of the stomach, where the food gets broken down. A bovine only has teeth on the lower jaw side, they lack upper incisors because they are herbivores. As they eat, they tear away at the grass, forage or hay and that goes into the rumen. The rumen then digests it to the next level. In that rumen is 'live' bacteria that creates the breakdown process, so the live bugs digest what the teeth could not.

So, with the first two drugs:

- You are building muscle with water
- You are building muscle with testosterone

But you also want that animal to be lazy and get fat.
Getting fat is where the rumen comes into the picture.

The reason for this coming in at the feedlot stage, is because the food changes to barley or U.S. corn. So when you change the diet of the animal to make it fat with no fibre involved, then all of a sudden you've got potential for coccidiosis. This is runny manure – the expelling of food. Meaning no digestion, it just goes straight through. So, in effect the runny manure is diarrhoea.

In the process, you've just gone and destroyed the one important part, where this live bacteria is supposed to be doing its job but it can't, because of the interference of the chemical toxins.

Well, there's another aspect to this bacteria that is forgotten about. The bacteria assists in the creation of the proper fatty acid profile of the animal, which we call the essential fatty acids or Conjugated Linoleic Acid (CLA). These fatty acids are healthy for our human system.

Why do we need to eat fatty acids?

The brain is a vital organ and its 'matter' is fat, with very little protein, this being the prion. This information was in the last chapter. The brain needs to be hydrated to remove toxins and heavy metals via the prion. The fatty oils are supporting the blood-brain barrier.

The CLA that naturally occurs in a raised bovine is one of the most concentrated God-given places where we can receive that whether it's from goats, sheep, oxen, bison, buffalo, yak and antelopes, to name a few.

So WHY would an industry sabotage a natural food source for humans?

WHY use unnatural processes?

WHY use chemicals, sprays and drugs?

These industries have been feeding the people altered, mutated and harmful food. So, a conventional method in this sense is playing with science which is not, it seems, for a positive intention.
I will give you an example.

"The meat fat composition can contribute to the onset of cardiovascular disease." Yes, it can when it's pumped full of steroids and additives because this is what goes from pasture-to-plate. Once the animal is slaughtered, the chemicals and drugs don't suddenly vanish, they live in the product itself and then you eat that meat and then your body is consuming that whole process! So yes, you could get cardiovascular issues with the stimulants already living in the meat you digest and absorb into your system.

Beef Cattle Research Council of Canada;
'Growth promotants are among the many sophisticated tools used by feedlots and other producers to raise more pounds of beef, more rapidly, using less feed, with decreased environmental impact, while maintaining high standards of animal health, carcass quality and food safety. Growth promotants include ionophores, growth implants, and beta-agonists. Health Canada's Veterinary Drug Directorate oversees the regulatory approval and oversight of these products in Canada's beef industry, and the Canadian Food Inspection Agency conducts random tissue tests for drug residues to ensure prescribed dosages and withdrawal times are adhered to'.

This is deception and lies.

It is not a sophisticated tool, it is unrefined and abhorrent.

We have trusted these laws and rules to obey and follow for too long and it's coming to an end. Our bodies deserve pure and natural food with no drugs.

Did you know that you can purchase meat from ranchers and farmers that are ethical?
I don't mean the modern terms for 'organic meat' or 'grass-fed meat' because what does that mean exactly?

A friend of mine Mischa Popoff, who is the author of the critically-acclaimed book,
'Is it Organic?' exposed the industry for what it is because there is so much bullshit out there! That's the bulldog rancher side of me coming out with ma swearin!

You don't think the producers or farmers lead the way, do you?

No, it's the government that is in the driver's seat of ALL food products.

So, I think it's time to end this chapter on a positive note.

Once again I will say, there is no blame or shame, just "move on outta the way now boys, we're taking over!"

Let's end with the **nonconventional** method.

This was my natural process, that took time to learn and I lost profits and sales along the way but it was worth it all in the end.

We used Welsh Black and Galloway Cattle, which are typically smaller northern hemisphere cattle. Meaning that they travelled across the seas from Scotland or Wales, Great Britain. They were animals that had hair and hide on them so that they would retain that inner fat, rather than putting fat on the outside to keep themselves warm. They would put on the marbling fat which is where that essential healthy fatty acid profile comes in.

I couldn't finish every animal, so I'd take a beating at the market. They weren't the cattle that I would promote so my profits would drop off. If I didn't stick to my marketing schedule, it was costly but if I could stick to the calendar programme, all was good. At that time, in our retail store, we drove the price up and said to the people "Listen, it costs us more to do it this way so try it and if you like it, then we'll come back." We were doing some really good business and you could feel it.

Feel it?

Yes, you can feel the quality of the meat. Not just with touch but with taste, texture and fulfilment. The richness of the meat was a luxury.

Have you ever bought meat and it shrinks?

I don't mean by a small amount but nearly half the size.

For example:
> Pork or bacon. You put large slices in the pan to fry and you can see it shrink in size before your eyes. This is because it's mainly water from the water retention, used in the drugs.

All meat, in essence, should keep its general size when cooked. I can only suggest that you try various products from different farmers. I have listed two options here. The first recommendation is with a farm that I have history with and the second is Danushia's recommendation from England.

***Beretta Farms, Canada** - *As part of a humane program, their cattle enjoy life on Canadian family farms that are known and trusted. Their cattle have access to graze on lush lands filled with green grass, clean water and fresh air with an abundance of space to roam.*

> *100% Canadian Cattle*
>
> *Raised without the use of antibiotics, hormones or steroids.*
>
> *Sustainable program from conception to consumption.*
>
> *Traceable back to their farm of origin.*
>
> *Humanely Raised.*

Third party verification and inspection are required by an accredited Certifying body, along with a thorough audit trail.

***Primal Meats, UK** - *Their meats are more than just sustainable, they're a vote towards a better future for their livestock and actively promote the regeneration of our planet and her ecosystems. They specialise in supporting those following 'healing diets' based on ancestral wisdom. Their beef, lamb, mutton and hogget are organically reared, 100% grass fed and carry the "Pasture for life" logo, providing reassurance of nutrient quality and traceability amongst a world of misleading "grass fed meat" products.*

This is our future

⋯back to my countryside ranch.

Our team had proved, undoubtedly, that microcosm can work with our little value chain and that's why we were ready to take it to the next level and build our own plant, hence my visit to China for my 'packing plant proposal'.

Nonconventional feedlots, allows the cattle to graze on pure grass and forage throughout their lives but in effect it's not efficient and can be very challenging. For Canada and the Northern USA, year round grazing is not possible due to the severe winter weather conditions. Though controlled grazing methods of this sort necessitate higher beef prices and the cattle take longer to reach market weight, it was always worth it!

I still believe that the U.S. is completely malnourished with no proper nutritional value and suitable nutrients, all because of the additives and artificial food, manipulated in everyday groceries. The food supply was and still is, currently, out of balance. But it is going to change and not over a decade or two but over the coming twelve months and ongoing.

Randy connecting with the his memories

As I said to you, I learned all aspects of the industry and I would even help out in the retail stores to sell our meat and I even wore a Santa hat on a few occasions! These were even some of my favourite experiences. If I had had the means financially to have survived back then, I would have loved to have volunteered to be with the people in the stores and connect one to one. Greeting customers. Listening to their stories.

Oh my gosh! I have so many stories but here's one that comes to mind.

A lady approached me with a child by her side. I was selling our homemade wieners that had no artificial fillings or additives in them, only pure beef, fats, conscious spices and smoked⋯mmmm!

They looked and tasted like a wiener but I know some folk in the world call them a 'frankfurter'.

This lady said to me "My son loves bacon and I know your wieners are nitrate-free but have you ever considered 'side pork'?"

We got our hogs from a specific farm that raised them to our similar standards, ethics and beliefs. Nitrates used can be full of synthetics and so we used more of a natural preservative like celery salts.

I told the lady "Well, that's what they make bacon out of, the side pork." Side pork is the belly of the animal and I brought some out to show her.

> Lady: "I know but it's not sliced."
>
> Me: "I know but I can slice it for you."

Her eyes filled with tears! She took a breath and said "Oh my god, where do you guys come from?"

I told her "This is what we want to offer the community. I know that you can see that the prices are pretty high because of our overheads and costs but we are doing our best!"

So, I sliced her up with some of that pork.

It was a special experience and she could see the passion and love in our service. That lovely lady is imprinted in my memory, one of many.

As you can see, I have a passion to give back to the community. To offer my services with an open heart. I have learned so much along the way and there is yet so much to do on this wonderful Earth.

So, with all that you have read about me and my experiences, do you think I have what it takes to be the Mayor of Calgary?

> "In economics, hope and faith coexist with great scientific pretension and also a deep desire for respectability."
> ~ John Kenneth Galbraith ~

15

City Council

"The capacity for erroneous belief is very great, especially where it coincides with convenience."

~ John Kenneth Galbraith ~

Generally, your city council has programs and services for YOU, the Public.

The list below includes the most commonly-offered services that your local City Councils offer you.

Environment
Waste

Recycling

Composting

Garbage

Water

Climate change

Building, Planning and Business
Improvement projects

Business and local economy

Building permits

Development of Land

Community

Public notices

Projects and studies

Heritage

Planning applications

Maps

Development

Flooding

Historic resources

Local policy plans

Business and local economy

Start

Grow

Maintain

Change

Improvements

Publications and Library

Employment

News

Events

Parks and Recreation

Arts and Culture

Transportation

Animal services

Taxes and Property

Social programmes/services

Bylaws and Public Safety

Investment and Support

Utility rates

And···Administration and record keeping of certificates, like marriages, deaths and birth, with local elections and local parishes!

Think about that.

Especially with what you have read in my book

As you can see it's a *big* list, *ready* for *big* change!

According to Wikipedia (01.05.2021)

The Calgary City Council is the legislative governing body that represents the citizens of Calgary. The council consists of 15 members: the chief elected official, titled the mayor, and 14 councillors. Naheed Nenshi was elected mayor in October 2010 as the city's 36th. Each of the 14 councillors represent one of the city's 14 wards (neighbourhoods).

The mayor of Calgary is elected through a citywide vote by all eligible voters. The mayor represents the interests of the city as a whole. The councillors are elected by the constituents of each ward. The councillors represent the interests of their respective wards. The mayor and councillors hold the office for 4-year terms. The last municipal election was held on October 16, 2017.

George Murdoch (April 29, 1850 – February 2, 1910) who was a Canadian politician, Alberta pioneer, saddle-maker, and the *first* mayor of Calgary, Alberta.

Term Began	*Term Ended*	*Time in Office*
December 4, 1884	October 21, 1886	1 year, 321 days

As of this writing, I, Randall Earl Kaiser, will be the 80th candidate to compete for the Mayorship of Calgary for 2021.

A final official list of candidates will be available after September 20, 2021.

When it comes to land mass, Canada is a massive country, even though I live in Calgary.

Would you believe me if I told you that there is a lot of 'waste land' in Canada?

What do I mean by waste land?

I don't mean waste that you put in trash or on a dumping ground but land that is wasted because it's not being used. We could feed the world with that acreage of land! We have so much abundance, it's not even funny.

Now I know I can appear calm, humorous, analytical and passionate but boy I've had such sadness, anger and frustration over the years around the subject of 'wasted land'!

Darn tootin! Ya betcha I have!

Sometimes, that inner rancher wants to yell out to the people and say, "Please everyone⋯open your eyes. This is insane!"

Well, there are times that I have done that but I can see that this method where I'm shouting from the rooftops doesn't always appeal to everyone! But that will never stop my journey of wanting **more** for the people. I believe they deserve it. That's why being the Mayor of Calgary became another realistic option for me.

I know I have the wisdom to teach and guide the councillors, councils, teachers, governments/leaders and the people, to gain a better understanding of what benefits we **can** have, with so much opportunity for improvement with regeneration and transformation.

So, the lands and our food produce is high on my list, as you may have gathered from previous chapters.

Not just for the businesses out there but also for households. Do you remember when I mentioned the gardens in chapter 2?

Since the lockdown, people have had the time to reconsider their lawns and garden space. To plant and expand the beauty of their yards or simply to create food. This is so important for us to take responsibility for our privileges. Now, you may be thinking "I know nothing about gardening" or "I don't like gardening" or "I don't have the time for gardening". Well, that's okay, it's only another approach. But some of you out there may *love* to have a garden full of herbs, vegetables or fruit and think the same thought patterns.   Here are some more offerings for you.

Could you hire someone to do this for you?

Could you make some exchange of service with someone?

Could you let someone use it for free where you both benefit?

Maybe another thought comes to mind for you, as you read this?!

It's about community and being part of something or put simply, it can give you the opportunity to create or propagate within your own space/property. Even if you have a window sill, you can propagate fresh herbs instead of going to buy a new bunch or pot, each time you shop.   You could save a fortune!

It's always beautiful to watch the sprouting of seeds grow up and turn into something you usually bought at the local grocery store. Or watching the root expand or the shoot blossom.

Start simple, if this is not something you generally do, just open your mind first and see if you feel like trying something new! We come back again to the conversation of 'conventional' and 'non-conventional' methods. Going back to the old ways that work and putting a modern spin on it. You could even make:

Paneer

Mozzarella

Sauerkraut

Kimchi

Kombucha

There is an endless list because of the luxury of our world cuisine.

We are lucky!

Reprogramming the mind! You never stay the same because you are always evolving. What you liked last year or a decade ago may be what you don't like now. It's a tool for expansion.

Income is another important factor for our modern world. You have read enough to hopefully gather that BIG change is required in this arena. Let's begin with state income/state benefits.

I am choosing not to get into the politics here but instead, a simple offering. **Increase** the amount given and change its title – for now I like to use 'comfort income'. This is so a person doesn't have to spend day-to-day, week-to-week, month-to-month in a constant state of limitation and surviving just to pay rent/mortgage/bills. The higher income opens the individual to an abundance of opportunities.

Comfort Income

Ignorance comes into this subject because it is believed if you are receiving something from the state, then you are a lower in standard or have less worth, as a human being.

Is this true?

Only if you believe in the 'misconception' of it.

Because of the creation of our modern times, there is ill-health, separation of family units, the elderly and disasters. Most of us are not immune to something changing in our lives, unexpectedly. And this financial support can be of benefit, especially if it is raised! For example:

* If you have an illness.
With the addition of 'worry for survival', then this added stress would contribute to declining one's health with speed. But if your income is increased, then you can detach from that stressfulness and focus on improvements, with better food or even participating in a 'form of healing modality.

* Family separation.

In survival, you are likely to be unable to focus enough attention on making clear decisions in order to create a more positive outcome, no matter what your situation. If your income is higher, your mind is clear so that you may come up with a better conclusion on the decisions you make, for yourself and your loved ones.

* Elderly.

Having worked your whole life to continue a *limited* life is very sad. It is a time to explore yourself and what you love experiencing in this life. A time to honour your life with support, healing alternatives, community and social aspects. This comes with a higher income.

* Disasters.

This could be from a sudden, uncontrollable crisis or a disastrous, personal choice. Having finances to support your transition through the emotional, physical and mental trauma and shock, is essential.

Now, if you have a higher income and you choose to abuse it and not be responsible, then okay. That's your personal choice which is called free-will. Because I believe the majority of people receiving this 'comfort' income would not abuse it because their lives have taken a turn for the better.

Municipal Taxes, or Council Taxes, have NO credibility and mislead the people to what the money contributes to.

Now, I'm not saying I disagree with the services offered to one's community but what I do disagree with, is the fraud and deception behind all of it.

An example of what I mean by this is, have you ever gone to a local council office and asked to see the budget of taxes for your community?

I would estimate that 99% of you said "No".

Is this because you...

Trust the system?

Just accept the system?

Never questioned the system?

Because as a taxpayer, you *should* be able to "trust the system".

Well yes, you should be able to trust the system but only if you are working with an "honest" system that gives the people the best of everything, in the first place!

Some of those services are generally supportive but some of those services require a reboot!

Presently;

§ Water supply is filled with fluoride, additives and chemicals that destroy its natural formation to hydrate and clean.

§ Road maintenance requires improved technology and no damage to the environments with materials currently used.

§ Police and Fire services can be upgraded to working from Common Law which is the reason why they take the oath to serve the people, not the governments.

§ Leisure and recreation projects to be expanded for all arenas, for all cultures. To create more options for day use, not the limitation to suit 9-5 workers. And this is a HUGE change to be addressed also! With hours of employment in society.

§ Libraries – some libraries are non-profit charities and not even connected to the councils. Nonetheless, improve the services offered for ALL.

§ Schools and educational services - Teaching true history and focusing on the human spirit and relationships, emotions, mental health and physical well-being. Recreating the theme of subjects (e.g. Mathematics - use numbers for real-life financials not equations that boggle the mind). Get the children to manifest their visions and goals and boost them to be business-minded, not just as a worker in the system.

§ Rubbish and waste collection to introduce better equipment for the workers and to create options to reduce or eliminate waste and recycling.

§ Environmental health is a big one! So many good changes are coming.

§ Fresh air to breath – build more parks, plant trees for recreational facilities.

§ Transport and highway services to be researched and developed for smarter and more efficient methods for comfort and easy passage. Do you remember me talking about the Bullet Train in China?

This is just a 'snippet' of some changes on HUGE subject matters.

It's not going to be an overnight 'quick fix' but it is going to be fixed. Humanity has had enough of oppression, inefficiency, control and slavery. We are heading for the 'death' of capitalism.

What is required is a *sustainable governance* that will benefit every human being on the planet towards freedom and liberation.

I will reiterate that I only desire to change the process from 'exploitation and manipulation' to 'consciousness and humanities'.

There never was lack and there never will be lack. Mother Earth provides for us all and never stops her magnificent support to **all**, who dwell on her plane-t.

Lack is man-made.

Lack is business.

Lack is a b(u)y-product of Capitalism.

Lack is a lie.

There is abundance for ALL.

    Water

    Food

    Oil

Money

Happiness

Peace

Laughter

Health

We have had enough of pain, suffering, illness and disease. Every one of us at some time has had an experience of ill health, no one seems to have escaped it. I guess that's part of being human too and how you overcome these obstacles to help others to help themselves. I have had illness too. My health has had many ups and downs but when I had a 'Near-Death Experience', my whole world changed!

"Tenure was originally invented to protect radical professors, those who challenged the accepted order. But we don't have such people anymore at the universities, and the reason is tenure. When the time comes to grant it nowadays, the radicals get screened out. That's its principal function. It's a very good system, really - keeps academic life at a decent level of tranquillity."

~ John Kenneth Galbraith - A Tenured Professor ~

16

Closer to God

"Good writing, and this is especially important in a subject such as economics, must also involve the reader in the matter at hand. It is not enough to explain. The images that are in the mind of the writer must be made to reappear in the mind of the reader, and it is the absence of this ability that causes much economic writing to be condemned, quite properly, as abstract."

~ John Kenneth Galbraith - Economics Peace and Laughter ~

I was born with, what some may call, a birth defect.

This deformity caused me so much pain as a baby, young child and going into my teenage years which followed me into adulthood.

This affliction was on my butt cheek!

The label for my torment was Congenital Hemangioma.

Congenital Haemangioma is made up of blood vessels that form incorrectly and multiply more than they should.

Large infantile Hemangiomas can sometimes be part of a syndrome called the PHACE syndrome.

Each letter stands for a condition:

P – Posterior fossa (a part of the brain) malformation

H – Hemangioma

A – Abnormal arteries in the brain or big blood vessels near the heart

C – Coarctation of the aorta - (A problem with the heart. The aorta is the large blood vessel that carries blood from the heart out to the body. Coarctation happens when part of the aorta is too narrow for enough blood to get through.)

E – Eye problems

This is my sensitive side, exposing such personal information but I know this is another message to reach someone, somewhere and somehow. A message of hope.

As a kid, every time I hit my arse with a 'bump', it was like someone had hit me with a hammer! From that 'thump' I would get a blood blister.

Have you ever had a blood blister?

Blood blisters come from blood vessels being damaged, without piercing the skin. They can look similar to a burn and can be either red or black as they are filled with blood instead of clear fluid.

Each time I bumped my butt, the blood blister would expand to the size of a mango! Yes, a mango sized blood blister on my butt cheek!

There were even times when it ruptured and swelled in size which was excruciating! When it got to this extreme point, the pain would bring on dreams. Like a part of me had to shut down and discard the unpleasant sensations.

I would float through space, feeling like a toothpick inside a marshmallow!

Then I would reach my hand out to Jesus Christ, who was stretching his hand out to me. He wore a beautiful blue robe with white attire underneath and his hair was brown in colour. He would say to me "Don't worry, just take my hand". Then I'd wake up!

The memories I had were of my mother, sitting by me and soothing me with a cloth on my forehead. I think that I must have shared the dream with my mother but I have no recollection of her opinion or words about my dream.

Over and over and over and over and over, I would have this repetitive dream in that state of pain, which lasted into my 20's.

As I remind myself of Jesus, it brings up a nice memory when I was growing up and how I loved my role as an altar boy. I got to ring the bell when it was time for Holy Communion but none of the other parts interested me.

My church was Roman Catholic and it was the usual indoctrination of fear, hell, fire and brimstone with words similar to "You are a sinner"; "Satan lives in you"; "Do not question the Church – Obey the Church"; "God sees everything".

Now, I look at all churches and religions differently.

I can agree somewhat that God does see everything but that's because:

God lives in me

God sees through my eyes

God hears through my ears

God tastes through my mouth

God touches through my skin

God feels through my soul

God loves me

I do not believe that God is a man who sits on a cloud threatening all life with fear and punishment. I regard God as a FORCE of UNIversal energy.

Uni = One

God is *all* life.

God is consciousness.

God is love.

God knows you're perfect, just as you are.

There is no sin.

Sin was a 'man-made' word, designed to condemn and frighten you.

There are just bad choices, negative thoughts and unnecessary actions.

It's only **you** that can find your way through life, to make better choices for yourself, as you rewire your brain to a positive mind-set. With these clear-cut actions, you will create a pathway of opportunity and expansion for your world.

DEVIL	**GOD**
Damage	Preserve
Crazy Thoughts	Balanced Thoughts
Accuse	Honour
Enemy	Friend
Deception	Truth
Fear	Love
Distract	Enlighten
Destroy	Create
Contamination	Purity

God is also a word and so is Yahweh, Allah, Buddha, Krishna, Shiva, Akal Murat, Consciousness, Infinite Spirit, Creator, Source or Light Force. But it is all ONE. I discovered interpretations and explanations in various languages from Hebrew, Aramaic, Greek, Egyptian, Latin and Elohim. Here are a few of those words with my own analysis and perception.

I believe these forces exist within us all.

Do you?

We can also be influenced by outside forces whether it's the universe, the elements, family, friends, leaders, mainstream news and media. But only you can decide which force you prefer to exist in yourself, in each moment.

I remember those forces of influence when I was even 14 years of age. I never cussed or swore but would say things like "dirty dog" or "Englebert Humperswearword".

Yes, that's exactly as I would say it "Englebert Humperswearword!"

Here's a little story for you.

My mother had an album by Englebert Humperdinck, and on the cover was an erotic picture with a woman bathed in cream, yikes! She was gorgeous. But because of God and the hell raisers, fire, brimstone and hell. I thought they were gonna take my 'dinck' straight off and I simply could not swear. Because Humper 'dinck' made me fear being punished. Other kids would make fun of me for not swearing properly but I perfected that technique with maturity!

The real truth though, was that I was fearful of playing with other children just for fun because with that freedom came pain. I could guarantee that I would somehow bump my butt, so I basically played on my own. I could never predict 'contact' from other kids and it was less stressful being on my own. I did enjoy it though, playing out in nature using my imagination and being careful, with no interference or worry.

At school, I did not play sports like hockey, baseball, etc. I was challenged because I really did want to rough and tumble with the other kids but the fear was far greater than the desire for fun. This continued throughout my teenage years and into adulthood.

I thought you had some feisty fights, Randall?

Well, yes this is true but I still had that fear of my butt being kicked and literally too! I always managed to protect this area and knew how to instinctively move my body position during a punch up. Sounds quite skilful actually! Now that I say it out loud. But I would rather get a punch in the cheek of my face, than the cheek of my butt! I could heal faster this way believe it or not. My face could recover much quicker than the alternative impact of pain and the swelling of blood blisters, which could take weeks to heal.

Generally, it was a trip to the hospital where I was prescribed drugs for the pain, with sleeping pills to dull out the discomfort and to take the pressure off and to reduce inflammation and find some peacefulness. But over time, I was beginning to get reactions to the prescription drugs and I noticed my skin's irritation and itchiness. I was starting a battle with pain and sleep versus tingling and prickling sensations.

My pain turned to anger.

Anger at the situation.

Anger at God.

The process of self-pity was consuming me - "Why me?".

I can openly admit now, that I was a furious young man, with many feelings of exasperation, frustration and limitation.

And when my father died when I was aged 21, I was pissed off at life!

After my parents had remarried (that's a whole other story!) My father, Earl Fredrick Kaiser, was diagnosed with stomach cancer. The conventional treatments, such as invasive removal of body parts and chemotherapy, *'butchered'* him. His mammal stature was reduced to 93lbs of skin and bone. I only knew this because I carried him in my arms out into the fields to look at the cattle and say goodbye. This was the last time that he ever saw those lands and animals. I took him to the car and gently positioned him for his drive to the hospital, I knew that he would never return. When I put him in the car, my mom left and I never went to visit him in the hospital again.

That's why I became so angry with this thing called God. I remember walking out into the fields and looking up at the sky, raising both arms up high with my fists clenched tightly and screaming out "*What kinda God would do that?*" I felt broken inside.

I lost my faith badly for many years because of my affliction and my dad. The anger took many years to settle down and it lingered in a lot of the things that I did. My thoughts and actions were reactive. I cannot say that it was prevalent in my relationships but my voice would get loud and my suppressed rage would expose itself. I was never violent or caused any physical harm to a female, ultimately, it was only to myself. The internal rage would ooze out of me, when I was around men, the brawling would inevitably commence. Thankfully, no weapons were ever used. The only item I can remember were smashed beer bottles! One time, one of those fractured bottles was coming in my direction and I slapped it outta his hand and punched him in the head but as he lay there doing the 'funky chicken', it actually scared the shit out of me. For the first time, I realised I could have killed a man and from that moment on, I knew that I could not continue this behaviour. Especially as violence in general was increasing around me and the idea of sorting myself out was also backed up by my buddy, who was always fast and on his feet in fights and generally won.

But sadly, he was in a situation where he punched a guy through a car window but he did not realise who else was in the car. They all got out and dragged him out of his car through the window and he was badly beaten up. This was back in the late 1970' and early 80's. Guns were starting to appear on the streets and you could feel the tension and extreme changes going on. Thankfully, I was ending my thug days as this was all beginning. My generation's weapons were our fists and our feet.

However, times were about to change!

Away from me for a moment, I want to connect with you.

Have you felt anger in your life?
To what?
To whom?
How did you deal with it?
How do you deal with it today?

Anger is a word that can be seen from many different angles. See which one of these emotions resonates best with you:

    Frustration

    Irritation

    Provocation

    Displeasure

    Annoyance

    Exasperation

    Animosity

    Antagonism

    Fury

    Rage

    Hatred

    Impatience

    Indignation

Outrage

Resentment

Jealousy

Irritable

Vexed

Mad

Freakin' Pissed!

All emotions *move* through us and *exist* around us.

When we hold onto these feelings and sensations, they build up and cause internal conflict that extends to external conflict. The emotions from the list of words described above, I will call 'anger' for short, just to keep it simple..

Anger is an experience.

Anger is not something to avoid or push away, as it's a human reality.

Anger can be:
Action
- Involvement
- Participation
- Exposure to
- Practicality

You cannot escape anger because it's real and true. It's just how you *deal* with your anger, with:
- Patience

Understanding

Maturity

Skill

Wisdom

There is more than one technique for everyone and everybody, to master your way through your anger. You just have to *want* to *find* that technique.

Suppressed anger can become a self-created *cage* or *trap* that can cause mayhem in our physical, mental and emotional body and it can affect the spiritual side of you too! There always comes a time, which this caged and entrapped side of yourself, is ready to unchain itself. To set the anger free.

$$Anger = pain = sadness = fear === finding\ love.$$

Anger is a deep unresolved pain, which stems from deep sadness that could not be felt because it hurt too much. The pain and sadness originated from fear.

Fear of what?
Fear of fun – what if I am not accepted?
Fear of death – losing someone you love.
Fear of love – risking your heart to be broken again.
Fear of abandonment – it hurt too much that that person didn't want you
Fear of rejection – what if I am wrong and make the same mistake again?
Fear of truth – being yourself without the judgement of others.
Fear of loneliness – surrounding yourself with false people and things.

Fear of playfulness – inner child memories.

Fear of hurting – from others.

Fear – Fear – Fear – Fear is everywhere and it stops us from feeling truly ALIVE and full of LIFE. It encroaches its way in and before you realise it, you are consumed with fear.

When you make the conscious decision connect with your anger and release the sadness from within, your hidden fears are acknowledged and you find love for yourself. You begin to fall in love with yourself. You get the opportunity to remember the parts of you and your life that were deeply buried, those 'buried parts' could have even been hiding for decades!

Our guardians forgot how to teach us how to love ourselves. We were only ever informed how to fall in love with someone or something outside of ourselves. Our loved ones forgot because they lost their love too.

Love = Freedom

Freeing yourself of your internal conflict and discarding them, layer by layer.

Don't worry my dear friends, you have all the time in the world to do this.

You just have to unravel those parts of yourself, to rediscover the magical human being that you are, through the eyes of God. Return to forgiveness.

Do you remember when I said to separate the word, for-give = give-for?

Forgiveness is freedom.

You give the love back to you.

Even when I have talked about my fights.

Fights are all around us and so anger exists, even in this historical timeline.
Anger at the 'elite'
Anger at the vaccine
Anger at people you call 'blind to the truth'
Anger at missed opportunities
Anger at limitation
Anger at deception
Anger at the 'systems'
…on and on and on and on.

We have been part of a creation that was false and led us into a criminal society but who are the true criminals?

The negative agendas have dangled us like puppets on a string with fighting one another, separating and segregating us.
   Colour
   Race
   Culture
   Tribe
   Language
   Religion

We have spent so much time fighting one another physically, mentally and emotionally, as though there is only one way to live life. The 'I am right and you are wrong' effect. But this is not true or real. It's all man-made.

When you believe you have no other choice, then you surrender yourself, put the white flag up and sink. Sink into those buried emotions. You always have the choice to unearth them. You simply need to allow yourself to do this.

As you know, ANGER is a powerful force.

Let's return to my anger, pain, drugs and the hospitals.

I had reached the age of 32 and I never had come across an alternative way to relieve the suffering of my butt!

This was about to change during a hospital visit in Edmonton, Alberta.

During my stay, Dr. Samuel Cox just happened to be working at the hospital that day and he came over to see me.

    Dr: I have taken these off people.

    Me: What?!

The doctor was referring to my Congenital Hemangioma.

I was surprised because no one had ever given me another option before. I was always led to believe by other medical specialists - "We could try to remove this for you Randall, but we may lose your leg!" So, with that threat, I feared going ahead with an operation.

I forgot to mention earlier, that it was not always internal swelling and pain but the ruptures could also move towards the skin and break through, causing infections. This was called 'outcropping'.

In previous times, I had some minor operations to seal this off with stitches but it was something that never went away. All of the measures were temporary.

Back to my conversation with Dr. Cox.

> Dr: Yes, I took one off a guy's arm, from his wrist to his shoulder. His arm is intact and only scarring remains. We removed it successfully for him.
>
> Me: Okay, let's fucking go for it!
>
> Dr: What do you mean 'let's go for it'?
>
> Me: Now, I'm ready! I don't know about you but I'm ready for the procedure. Are you here for a while?
>
> Dr: Well, I come and go. But to go ahead with this, we must begin with the correct process. I will have to examine you to determine whether it's embedded in your muscle tissue or other areas. We can take it on if all is well to do so, that's if you're interested?
>
> Me: Of course, I'm interested! I already said so.

Over the coming months, I was examined with x-rays and ultrasound. I had to get the swelling reduced in size, as this took time and I was also making some positive changes around me in my life with people and lifestyle options.

My big operation day arrived!

I was in surgery for up to five hours and when all was complete, I ended up sleeping through the night. The next morning, I awoke and saw that I was hooked up to an IV. I needed to go to the washroom, so I moved one leg and I thought to myself "Gee, that's working fine! I'll go on my own." I carefully made my way over and all was well. When I returned to my bed, a doctor knocked on the door and asked me how I was doing. "Buddy, this is amazing! My leg feels perfect and I barely feel any pain. Can I go home?" The doctor replied "Well, we'll see what Dr. Cox thinks, when he visits you later."

I knew that my sister was visiting me later on, so I thought this would probably work out fine.

Time passed and the IV had been removed. The medical team believed that I did not need it anymore and all appeared to be functioning well, according to them. This was great news.

I needed to take a leak again, so I made my way to the washroom, this time without the IV.

As I was at the sink, I raised my eyes and saw my face in the mirror and I stared curiously, as I saw huge beads of sweat coming out of my forehead, they were the size of peas!

With that, I knew I had to make my way back to the bed but after a few steps, I collapsed like a lead weight in a heap on the floor. I had some consciousness and I remember voices and the staff attending to me quickly and lifting me off the floor onto the bed. As they were taking over, I started to disappear. Leaving everyone and everything and going somewhere, like a void. It was painless. I did not know what was going on but I was fearless and my brain was still in some thought. I did not float above or outside of my body but I knew that I had left my physical body. I went through a dream state and saw all of the good things in my life. I was peaceful and I had a sense of Karma. It was like "If I go now, I'll have had a good life."

There was no 'time'
It was all 'space'

I was told later by the medical team, that the wound had been collecting the blood as I slept, after the procedure. By the time I had gone to the washroom a second time, the stitches could not hold the blood in any longer and it went from oozing out of my body to a sudden 'gush' and that's when I collapsed. The only thing that was keeping my heart going after the operation was the intravenous tube, but it had been removed.

As they replaced the IV back into my body, slowly but surely, I started to see again and I came back! Some call this a Near Death Experience

(NDE). Over the next few days I received nine units of blood in what I called a complete oil change.

I had another trip to the hospital after this episode and all that remains physically, is a scar that looks like a shark bite!

But the change was not just physical, this experience had changed my 'mind'. It took away the fear of dying and death and lots of other fears, which I had lived with for decades. The change was profound, on all levels physical, emotional, mental and spiritual. This powerful episode changed my whole life and my relationship with myself and others.

I was prescribed Lithium after this exposure to the afterlife because I found some things very challenging between the physical world and the non-physical universe. I continued with this medication for another decade and I have no regrets. That was about 20 years ago now. Everything comes into our life for a reason and it can be years before we find the full 'value' in a lesson or experience.

Maybe, even some of my concussions from my fighting days and getting punched in the head attributed to my mental health, as it must affect the mind somehow? Not just through imbalances in mentality but biologically and in the brain's chemistry. Ultimately, it's trauma to the head.

The reason why I came off Lithium after ten years, was because during one of my doctor's visits, I was diagnosed with *'liver cancer'*. This caused me to drop the drug and go to a naturopath, which turned my world around even more?

Now, I feel like I could live forever! I feel at my strongest physically, energetically, emotionally and mentality, more now than I have ever felt before. I may be sixty years old but I feel half that age.

The naturopath came into my life because my son had some issues and was doing a prescribed 'liver cleanse', it was all synchronised events. I thought I would give it a go and it worked well for me and I still continue with these cleanses to this day. That naturopath recognised that I had liver cancer within 90 minutes of our meeting and I hadn't told him anything about the disease!

He simply said "We've got this Randall! Think 'Perfect Health'".

And I did for many months, alongside the liver cleanses and I do remember some remedies he issued to me, Milk Thistle and Sweet Clover to name a few!

I am not recommending you do anything that I did, I advise research first and follow your gut instincts. The right path is what is perfect for you.

I had such anger, pain, conflict, fights and death to contend with for decades and that energy had to flow somewhere and it did, as my story shows.

In Eastern medicine, the Liver is the 'seat' of anger.

It all started with my childhood.

"Wealth is the relentless enemy of understanding"

~ John Kenneth Galbraith - The Affluent Society ~

17
Splitting Adams

"I would now, however, more strongly emphasize, and especially as to the United States, the inequality in income and that it is getting worse—that the poor remain poor and the command of income by those in the top income brackets is increasing egregiously. So is the political eloquence and power by which that income is defended. This I did not foresee."

~ *John Kenneth Galbraith - The Affluent Society* ~

Everything begins in childhood.

It's our ancestry and we evolve through time.

I recently spoke with my Uncle Ken who has reached his 9th decade in life and he talked to me about Adam.

Adam is my father's ancestral lineage.

Adam was my great Grandfather.

Adam was also my great, great Grandfather.

The two Adam's were father and son and they were big farmers in agriculture. They had accumulated their wealth in Europe, where they originated from before they found a new homeland in South America. The family line then decided to move up to Canada. My personal research uncovered stories about them both. I discovered that my lineage went back to being one of the *biggest* farmers in Wetaskiwin, Alberta. They raised cattle, hogs, chickens and I think even ducks! Their business was big enough that they had been able to hire a lot of native people to work on the land.

My paternal Grandmother told me that they had to change their surname because they could not get into Canada and so that was how Kaiser was born. Kaiser is a typical German name but I feel we are more linked to the Tartarian and Prussian bloodlines.

Worldwide, surnames have evolved over centuries, as a way to sort people into groups - by occupation, place of origin, clan affiliation, patronage, parentage, adoption, and even physical characteristics (like red hair).

Tartaria is the remnants of the Christian era under the format brought by Jesus. There is great evidence of Jesus's visits to Scotland and his connection to the Celts and the Druids.

Prussian was originally 'Preussen' (German) referred to by the geographical area settlement as the Baltic tribe, the Pruzzen. This area later became the Duchy of Preussen (Prussia), a Polish Kingdom. The Baltic tribe or Baltic people, were the last Pagans of Europe.

My late Grandmother suggested that our original surname was something similar to Cotash/Costash. For me, it has a Gaelic resonance. Maybe the future might take me across the waters to find out!

The two Adams, father and son, were very close. But sadly my great Grandfather also died young in a car accident, like my father.

One day, Adam was taking cattle to the city of Edmonton to sell his produce and as he was overtaking another vehicle in his one tonne truck, he hit the ditch.

My father was a unique man when compared to his other family members. He had a balanced nature and I feel he passed this trait down to me. I do believe he was the only child of his family to have been born naturally at home and not in any hospital surroundings. I wonder if this was the start of his childhood. To be born in homely surroundings with support of family members.

Our modern centres have formed into an assembly distribution line of mothers, bringing the baby into a world full of noise, intense lighting and unnatural medication. With forced labour that includes unnecessary and life-threatening operations, which is mechanical and clinical and sometimes, inhumane.

This is changing and I feel, this will return to the beautiful and essential entry into this world, which is with gentleness, kindness, patience and purity. Both what the mother and baby deserve. There are ways to create a blessed event for your baby during birth which is all natural, from Doulas to Hypno-birthing. These are just some methods and I know more and more will crop up in the future.

Having any type of birth trauma, impacts on the cells and atoms of the physical body and this energy is simply, Post-Traumatic Stress Disorder (PTSD).

Yes, it is a Dis-Order!

Dis = acronym.

Acronym = terminology.

Dis = apart * away from.

Order = structure * plan.

I see this as a separation of something that needs realigning.

So, stress and shock, if left untreated or ignored, will remain in the cells of the body, even if your mind has chosen to separate the shock. This reminds me of when my pain was excruciating and my body separated my mind from the pain, which led me to dream of Jesus reaching out his hand.

The mind and body seem to have their own unique emotional and spiritual side. It's like they find their own harmony to survive when under stress.

But you can resolve these traumas and memories, there are so many healing modalities out there to support you through the process.

Imprinting is an important aspect of life and arriving in the world needs to be something special, as its God's celebration, as a pure soul enters the wonders of Mother Earth. My own imprint as a child is simply a part of my personality. We all have this imprinting. Our brains are a programme and we see what we choose to believe. We then put words and language to that. For example; "a 'cow' makes the sound 'moo'" – "the 'sky' is 'blue'".

Imprinting can be positive or negative.

Imprinting is partly programming.

A memory comes to mind.

As a little boy, my parents would spank me when I misbehaved. I mainly got into trouble for fighting with my older sister. We would get punished by being spanked, to teach us how to be peaceful. Yes, I know this is ironic but stick with me.

When my father smacked me, I remember looking into his face and I knew that he felt bad doing this to me. I never saw any tears in his eyes but something else. I felt it was not to control me but train me.

One memorable incident when I was aged 4/5 years, was on a car journey. My sister and I were arguing in the back seat. Dad kept saying to us both, "Keep it up and you'll be sitting on the side of the highway and I'll leave you there!"

We continued and then he suddenly stopped the car!

He pulled us both out of the car and sat us down on the side of the road and got back in the car to drive away!

My sister just sat there with her arms crossed and I was hanging onto the door handle of the car, bawling my eyes out until he stopped the car.

This was his 'training'. He did teach me something. To find middle ground in situations, to compromise in fights or arguments. And I still think in those terms today, so in an ironic way, I say 'Thank You' to my mother and father for that early 'imprinting', that serves me now.

Programming can come through experiences at school.

I didn't pay attention until Grade 6 and I actually won an award for the 'Best Student'. It certainly boosted my ego and confidence and yes, I also got a bit 'cocky' about it, which did piss some of the other students off!

By the time I got into Grade 7-8-9, I started to think independently "What the fuck do I need this for?" I would follow the rules and pass my exams which moved me onto high school, which was even worse! My attitude was changing and when I arrived home for lunch at midday, I would often turn the television on and see what was on at the 'Matinee Theatre' after I finished eating my food. I would then opt for a beer and a movie, instead of school! At this time, I was living with my father, as my parents had separated. I don't have many memories of my dad but I loved his nickname 'Squirrel'!

I grew up fast in a short space of time with my father and he gave me so much freedom. I even had my own car at the age of 15! I know nothing about the license or insurance, I left that to my dad. I had a few wild years with him, drinking, partying and watching movies!

I managed to scrape my way through high school and receive my Matric diploma or maybe it was a 'Matrix' diploma! ;-)

My mother Pearl Kaiser nee Hogg, was so proud of me!

Actually my mother was proud of all of us! Whenever she had a conversation, she would tell whoever she was talking to how amazing we were, she exuded such delight and enthusiasm. It was actually over the top!

Dad (aka - 'Squirrel')

My graduation was a special memory as my mother and father had divorced when I was 14, due to many ups and downs. They had been separated for three years and during this celebration, they winked at each other and ended up re-marrying. So Pearl and Earl reunited! But then shortly after their wedding, my father was diagnosed with the cancer and then he fuckin' croaked it!

A tragic comedy, I guess.

My mother was an extremely positive woman, no matter what life threw her way. She rarely swore and did not like to use nasty and negative words about people or things in life. I just remember her loving nature. She was not indoctrinated either and was a free-

Mum & Dad - Re-married

thinking woman.

My mother left this world to go and find some happiness among the stars in 2012. She was diagnosed with a brain tumour and once again the medical industry *'butchered'* her too.

I tried to talk to her about alternative methods of healing and supportive measures but the pain was too much for her and she felt to continue with the conventional ways. She was operated on and surprisingly, this changed her cognitive behaviour. She became sweet and jolly again like she had been many years earlier. This procedure created a softness that I remember from long ago. It was surreal. My mother was positive but the pain would make her angry and I did actually hear the odd profanity coming out of her mouth!

- During that time, a memory from school studies popped up for me. The memory of Phineas Gage.

Have you heard of him?

As a foreman in construction, he had a severe accident, when an iron rod went completely into the top of his skull and through his face. This story comes up because he completely changed personality, from an angry person to a *"socially far better adapted"* human being. –

So, when my poor mother had the operation on her frontal lobe, all the anger vanished and most of the time all she did was just smile during the time she had left. This was for about 8-10 months and we saw this beauty within her return. I did give her a surprise, though!

A couple of months before she passed away, we took her to the top of a hill, in the snow and put her on a toboggan and pushed her down! She glided down the hill and tumbled on the snow at the bottom. "Oh my God!" as I went running to lift her up and she just laughed and laughed and said that she hasn't had so much fun in her life, until now.

I loved her then and still love her now.

A few months ago, I asked my sister if she had any photographs of dad and she sent me some over. I felt it was time to tell him "Fuck dad, I've made it! There's no turning back now. I'm gonna be in a position to help a LOT of people!" It was not out of pride or ownership of 'something' but in honour to myself, to keep going. To continue to follow my 'signs' and to go where others fear to tread.

I like to meditate as this calms my soul and keeps me focused and clear-headed. I have started to add gratitude and honour to my ancestors when I pray in thought or out loud. I now say my parents' name out loud because even though they were my parents, they were individuals. They were human souls on Earth. The 'roles' they played out as father and mother, was an addition to their lives. I may not be able to connect with them on the 'spirit' side but for a moment in time, I respect them by saying their name and in that exact moment, they are with me by my side.

I then smile with pure love and gratitude.

I smile as I know my ancestors and loved ones love me.

Love is not goofy, sissy or a weakness.

Love is the greatest power you will ever have the privilege to own.

With Peace, Harmony, Love, Abundance and Freedom, Everyday on My Mind.

Abundance, Sovereignty, Health, Love and EUPHORIA for ALL!

Love ya!

"The modern conservative is not even especially modern. He is engaged, on the contrary, in one of man's oldest, best financed, most applauded, and, on the whole, least successful exercises in moral philosophy. That is the search for a superior moral justification for selfishness. It is an exercise which always involves a certain number of internal contradictions and even a few absurdities."

~ John Kenneth Galbraith

A Promise

I am making a promise to you, with the belief in my heart and soul.

That you *will* see the Good in People *rise up* to aid Humanity.

I feel privileged to be here in these current times, through the chaos, pain, shock and trauma of the reality, before our very eyes.

This sounds strange but the beauty that is here which is expanding bigger and faster for us all to see, touch and feel, is Biblical! We are part of the greatest Historical periods over thousands upon thousands of years of history, on this Earth. It will continue to become widespread through books, films and education to all, for our future times.

The dark agenda has shone the light on earth for *goodness* and *greatness*.

From my heart to yours and all of humanity, I thank you for being alive!

Afterword

My contribution from the soul.

Danushia, William and myself started this book. A short chapter in our lives with three unique and individual wishes and one overall goal of completing a book that will help many people, with their private stories

Each of us having ideas on how this book would look and each having experience in collaboration. In the end, it may not be each of our perfect vision, but on a collective basis, IT is perfect. Since everything in life is truly perfect and moving towards being complete

If we did not have challenges, we would not learn how to Love the hell out of those challenges and end where everything started and is complete

In Love

Please consider these thoughts in your private, and our collective human experience and know that ALL is GoOd

ALL is Love

Steinbeck, from 'The grapes of Wrath', says;

There ain't no sin and there ain't no virtue

There's just stuff people do

However

Aramaic defines sin as "missing the mark" and Satan, as crazy thoughts

So if we simply think and act on our loving thoughts; and in fact love everyone and everything every day, we can mostly avoid sin and Satan

And trust the great mystery, Holy Spirit to grant us our wishes

With Love

Randall

Aramaic Prayer

Oh Cosmic Breather of all radiance and vibration

Soften the ground of my being and carve out a space within me where presence can abide. Fill me with creativity so that I may be empowered to bear the fruit of *Our* Mission

Let each of my actions bear fruit in accordance with our desire of "Abundance, Sovereignty, and Health and Love and Euphoria for ALL"

Endow me with the wisdom to produce and Share what each being needs to grow and flourish

Thank you for untying the last tangled thread of destiny that bound me, as I release others from the entanglement of past mistakes

I love you

I'm sorry

Please forgive me

Thank you

My Pleasure to Share, Serve, and Give

Do not let me be seduced by that which would divert me from our true purpose, but illuminate the opportunities of the present moment

For we are the ground and the fruitful vision, the birth power and fulfilment, as all is gathered and made whole once again….

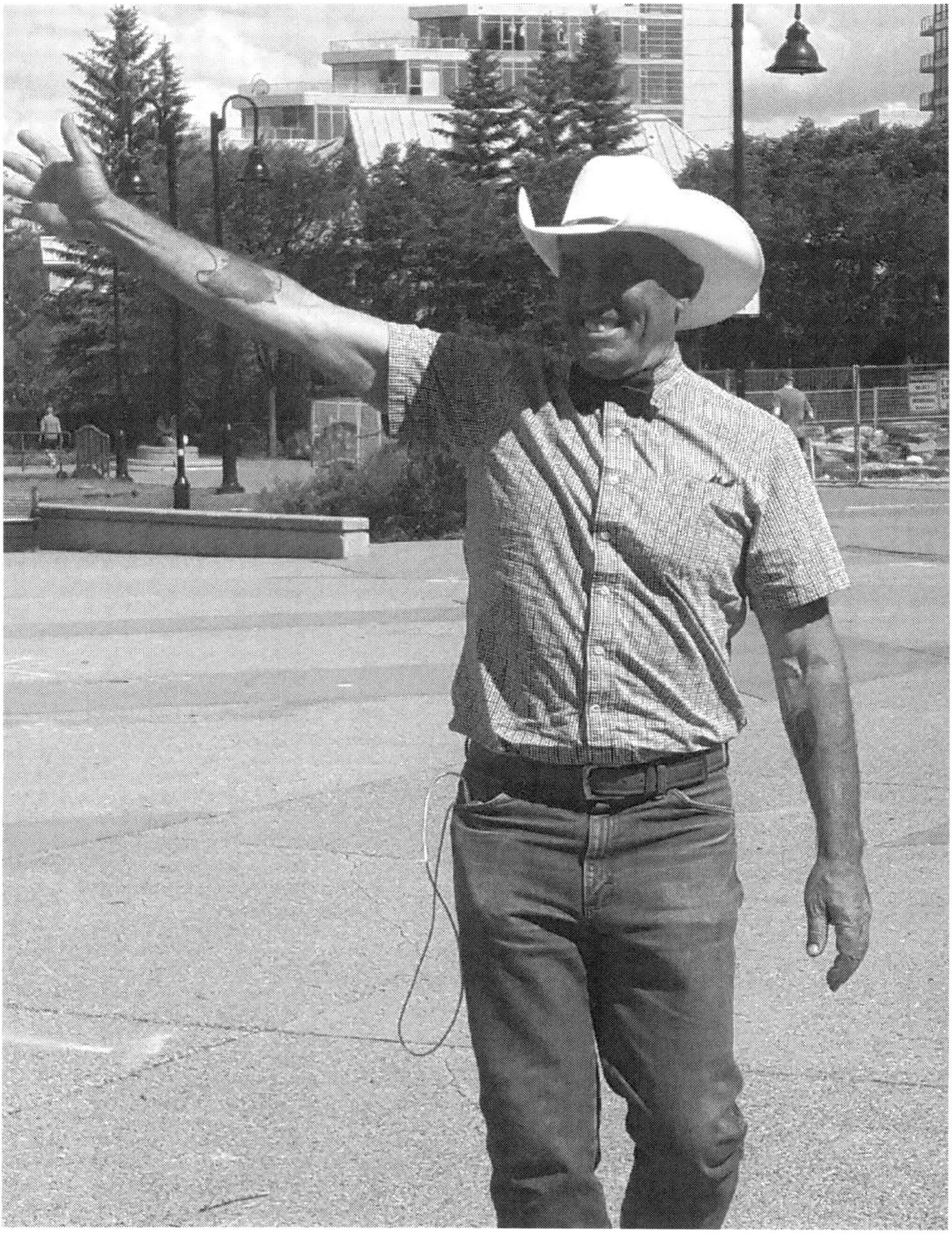

Public & Banking

Debt

is just an

Illusion

Personal Acknowledgements

I wish to give special thanks to each and every one of you and I am so grateful to you, thank you!

In no particular order:

Danushia Kaczmarek
William Ladic
Lee Mudders
Andrea Grace
Ida Civiero
Jim
Jennie Byers
Leah Mattinson
Benjamin Mensah
Hamid & Nadea
Aida Farhat
Roman Light
Gregory Hallett
Huna Flash
Anna Von Reitz
President Rodrigo Roa Duterte
Sara Duterte
Angelito Mallonga
General Carlos Malana
Paul Adolph Volcker
Jimmy Carter
Ronald Reagan
Richard Dohner
Margaret Kocsis
Queen Legaspi
Minnie Rose
Gold'en girls
Eddy
Henry
Sino
Sacha Stone
Neil Keenan
Raveeroj Rithchoteanan
Arthur Tugade
Bauer Rauthschild
Fred
Kingpin

Jason
Lisa
John Ioannidis
Dr. Michael Yeadon
Mark Purdy
Mischa Popoff
Dr. Samuel Cox
Grandmother
Grandfather Adam
Great Grandfather Adam
Earl Fredrick Kaiser
Pearl Hogg

Other Acknowledgements

Grateful Acknowledgements is made for the use of the following:

John Kenneth Galbraith Quotes
October 15, 1908 - April 29, 2006
Economist, diplomat, public official and intellectual.
A leading proponent of 20th-century American liberalism.
His books on economic topics were bestsellers from the 1950's through the 2000's.

Bibliography:

Ownership of the People - Osborne's Concise Law Dictionary, Ninth edition.
De-program.org
Awakened UK
Thoughtco.com
JFK Library Organisation
Beef Cattle Research Council of Canada
The Calgary City Council

Wikipedia
FinGlobal
Moneyland
Federal Reserve
HMRC
HM Treasury
Citibank Group
The Pushback
Oracle Films
Luke Andrews - Daily Mail
Swissindo News
Global News Canada
Think Tank
Beretta Farms, Canada
Primal Meats, UK
Bibi Bacchus

Public & Banking Debt is just an Illusion

Printed in Great Britain
by Amazon